Contents

Your Welsh Heritage
From Ancient Times to the Present

by

Peter N. Williams

ISBN: 978-0-557-43738-2

The Unitary Authorities of Wales

In 1996 the old 13 counties (Anglesey, Caernarfon, Flint, Denbigh, Radnor, Montgomery, Brecon, Monmouth, Glamorgan, Pembroke, Carmarthen, Cardigan, and Merioneth) were reorganized into 22 new counties or county boroughs (unitary authorities) reflecting population densities.

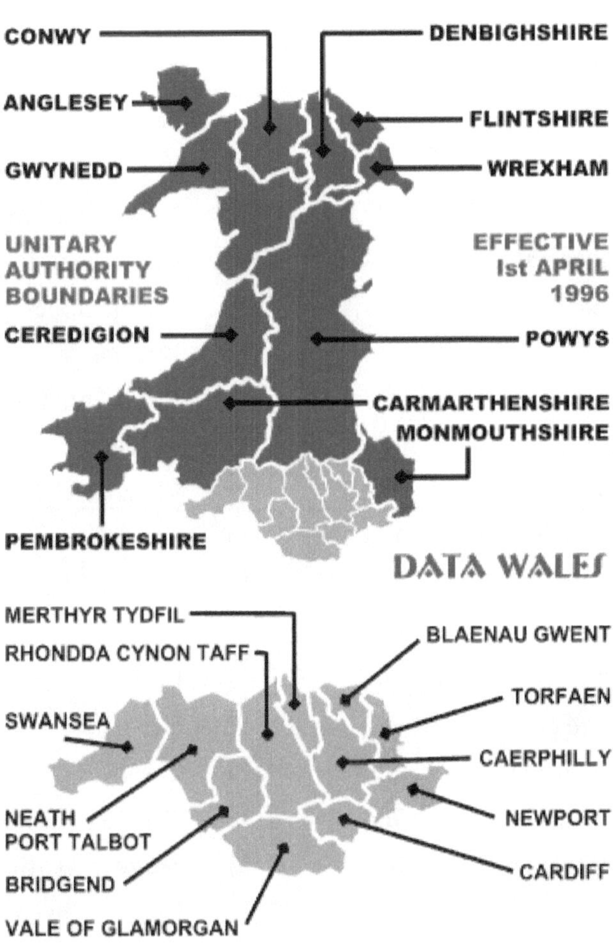

County and County Boroughs: Rankings by Population and Size

Rank		Population (in 1000's)			Size (in sq. miles)
1	Cardiff	320.9	1	Powys	6,196
2	Rhondda Cynon Taff	240.4	2	Gwynedd	2,548
3	Swansea	229.5	3	Carmarthenshire	2,394
4	Caerphilly	169.6	4	Ceredigion	1,795
5	Carmarthenshire	169.0	5	Pembrokeshire	1,589
6	Flintshire	147.0	6	Conwy	1,130
7	Newport	139.2	7	Monmouthshire	850
8	Neath Port Talbot	138.8	8	Denbighshire	838
9	Bridgend	131.4	9	Isle of Anglesey	714
10	Powys	126.0	10	Wrexham	504
11	Wrexham	125.2	11	Neath Port Talbot	442
12	Vale of Glamorgan	121.3	12	Flintshire	438
13	Gwynedd	117.5	13	Rhondda C.T.	424
14	Pembrokeshire	113.7	14	Swansea	378
15	Conwy	111.9	15	Vale of Glamorgan	331
16	Denbighshire	90.5	16	Caerphilly	278
17	Torfaen	90.2	17	Bridgend	251
18	Monmouthshire	86.3	18	Newport	190
19	Blaenau Gwent	72.0	19	Cardiff	140
20	Ceredigion	70.7	20	Torfaen	126
21	Isle of Anglesey	65.4	21	Merthyr Tydfil	111
22	Merthyr Tydfil	57.0	22	Blaenau Gwent	109

Chapter One: Introducing the Homeland

The irregular-shaped western peninsula of middle Britain that is known as Wales (Cymru) is only some 40 miles wide at its narrowest and 100 miles across at its widest. Its maximum length is only 140 miles. Occupying a little over 8 per cent of the total area of the United Kingdom of Great Britain and Northern Ireland, it has 5 percent of the population.

Wales is a mountainous land; one quarter of the country is over 1.000 feet high. It has 168 summits over 2,000 feet and 15 over 3,000 feet. The main mountain ranges are Snowdonia (depicted) and Cader Idris in the North, and the Brecon Beacons in the South. In Snowdonia, *Yr Wyddfa (Snowdon)* is 3,560 feet in height; and in the Beacons, *Pen y Fan* reaches 2,907 feet.

Three major British rivers, the Dee, the Severn, and the Wye have their beginnings in the Welsh hills. *Pistyll Rhaeadr*, at 240 ft, is the highest waterfall in Britain south of Scotland. Snowdon records the highest rainfall in the British Isles with an average of 180 inches per annum (245 inches were once recorded high on its slopes).

Wales is justly proud of its three National Parks: Snowdonia (838 square miles); the Pembrokeshire Coast (225 square miles); and the Brecon Beacons (519 square miles). Forty percent of the whole Welsh coastline has been designated as Heritage Coast areas. The Gower Peninsula in the South was chosen as Britain's first Area of Outstanding Beauty.

Agriculture takes up 81 percent of the land, woodland 12 percent, and urban areas only 7 percent. The sand dunes at Merthyr Mawr, Mid

Glamorgan, over 200 feet in height, are the second highest dunes in Europe.

In 1974 the old, historic thirteen counties of Wales were re-organized according to their share of the total population of three million. The counties of Flintshire and Denbighshire combined to form Clwyd. Anglesey, Merioneth and Caernarfonshire became Gwynedd. Montgomery, Radnor and Brecon united to form Powys. Cardigan, Carmarthen and Pembroke were joined together to form Dyfed Monmouthshire remained as Gwent; and heavily populated Glamorganshire was divided into South, Mid, and West Glamorgan.

In 1996, further changes took place, leaving Wales with 22 unitary authorities that vary greatly by size and population. Powys, for example, has more than fifty times the area of Blaenau Gwent. Cardiff's population is more than ten percent of Wales as a whole; that of Merthyr is less than 2 percent of the total.

Cardiff (Caerdydd) is the capital city of Wales, given that title in 1955. Now designated as a county, its area is 140 sq. km, with a population of over 320,000. The vibrant city, one of Europe's fastest-growing and fastest developing, is home to the fabulous Millenium Stadium at historic Arms Park; the National Assembly, a Norman and Victorian Castle, an impressive Civic Center (picture); the National Museum of Wales (both in the city itself and at Llandaff, where the National Welsh Folk Museum ranks with Europe's best).

In what was Bute Town, the old docks area, once known as *Tiger Bay*, with an unsavory reputation, has been transformed into a vibrant community of government buildings, entertainment complexes, attractive apartments, and a plethora of new, exciting ethnic restaurants. The barrage across the Bay has given a total new look to the waterfront. The Wales Millennium Centre has become an international receiving house for opera, ballet, dance and musicals. It also houses under one roof seven diverse and exciting cultural organizations, including the Welsh National Opera Company.

Swansea (Abertawe), some fifty miles West of Cardiff, is the second largest Welsh city (c. 235,000). It has managed to shake off the shackles of a grimy, industrial past (and massive destruction in World War 11) to emerge as a bright, attractive city. Situated on a magnificent bay, Swansea also lies at the edge of the unspoiled Gower Peninsula, the first area of Britain designated as one of Natural Beauty. The old docks area is now a bustling, modern marina, where pride of place is given to the Welsh Industrial and Maritime Museum, surrounded by up-scale apartments, restaurants and hotels. The city is also home of the Welsh National Pool, a training facility for Olympic swimmers. Its modern, stylistic Guildhall houses the Frank Brangwyn murals, the largest set of paintings in Britain.

The third largest city in Wales is Newport (Casnewydd) in mostly English-speaking Monmouthshire (Gwent). With a population of approximately 130,000, the city is the home of St. Woolos Cathedral, overlooking the bustling market town, with its Norman Castle; Westgate Square (scene of the famous Newport Rising of 1839); and the unique Transporter Bridge, a "suspended ferry," one of only two such bridges in Britain.

Mid-Wales boasts Aberystwyth, the principal centre of Welsh culture, and the home of the first University College of Wales (depicted), founded by public subscription in 1872, that was to have a profound influence on the culture, language, and consciousness of the nation. High above town on Constitution Hill is the Camera Obscura, a rare survivor of Victorian Wales, reached by a 19th century electric cliff railway. On Penglais Hill is the splendid National Library of Wales, founded in 1907 (like the University, much of the financing came from public subscription).

Wrexham (Wrecsam) is the largest town in North Wales, serving a wide area as a market town and fast-growing center of high technology based on Glyndwr University. Its magnificent St. Giles Parish Church, reached by the wrought iron gates of the famous Davies brothers of nearby Chirk, has a replica at New Haven, Connecticut. Elihu Yale, founder of the American university that bears his name, is buried in the churchyard.

Llandudno is the largest resort town in Wales. Sheltered by two great headlands, it has two beaches, a wonderful promenade, first-rate hotels, the Theatre of North Wales, and a cable car and tramway to the top of the Great Orme (where Bronze Age copper mines can be explored). Not too far from Llandudno, in the mountainous Northwest, underground tours can be enjoyed at the great slate quarrying district of Blaenau Ffestiniog, where vast accumulations of waste slate testify to the amount of industry once carried on in that mostly Welsh speaking district.

In the Northwest, Caernarfon, in Gwynedd, was a Roman garrison town with remains of their presence at the fort of Segontium.

Dominated by the mighty castle of Edward 1st, the town remains a bastion of Welsh language and culture. It has been designated a World Heritage Site. In industrial Northeast Wales, Flint is the home of the first of the many castles ordered built by Edward 1 to keep a stranglehold on the people of Wales (depicted). Rhuddlan Castle is a second mighty Edwardian stronghold, where even the River Clwyd was diverted to bring supplies to the English garrison. *The Statute of Rhuddlan* (The Statute of Wales) was enacted here in 1284 to introduce the English legal system following the death of Prince Llywelyn ap Gruffudd.

Carmarthen (Caerfyrddyn), in the Southwest, was once the largest town in Wales. Named after the Welsh mythologcal figure Merlin (Merddyn), it was here, at the Ivy Bush Inn, the Gorsedd of Bards first met in 1819. Situated high on the banks of the Towy, with many historic buildings, it is an attractive town that serves as a market for a wide area. In the southwest is Laugharne, where internationally known Dylan Thomas wrote much of his poetry in his boathouse on the shores of the estuary. Nearby Pendine Sands is a former site of world racing car records. Farther west, in Pembrokeshire, is found the largest Cromlech in Wales (Pentre

Ifan) and the quarry from which the mysterious blue stones of Stonehenge were transported.

In Southeast Wales, one of the largest castles in Europe, second in size only to Windsor, is to be found at Caerphilly, a few miles north of Cardiff. The mighty Norman fortress, completely dominating the former cheese-making town, covers 30 acres with impenetrable water defenses. Blaenavon Iron Works, in Gwent, a World Heritage Site, preserves the heritage of the area's great iron and coal industries, while the Big Pit Mining Museum in nearby Blaenau offers an unusual, exciting educational experience at the underground tours of the old mine workings

Chapter Two: The Long, Troubled Road to the National Assembly

The principality of Wales was totally absorbed into the Kingdom of Great Britain in 1536 by the Act of Union. It had to wait until 1997 to receive some form of self-government (alas, without revenue-raising powers) when the National Assembly came into being. A directly elected body with 60 members, the Assembly, housed on Cardiff Bay, has been given the responsibility for carrying out government policies and public services in Wales. It had been a long, troubled journey much of which is written in its landscape.

Prehistoric man left his mark in the huge burial chambers that are found everywhere (depicted is Pentre Ifan). Iron Age man built hilltop forts and dwellings; Bronze Age man mined for copper; the Romans came in the lst Century A.D. to build towns, military encampments, and amphitheatres; they also mined for gold, lead, and other precious metals. They destroyed the ancient religion of Druidism and introduced Christianity. After their withdrawal from Britain in the early 5th century, there followed hundreds of years of warfare between the native Romano-British Christians, who called themselves *Cymry*, and the invading Anglo-Saxon Pagans, eventually becoming known as *English.*

In the 8th Century, Wales was separated from England by a great embankment and ditch known as Offa's Dyke, named for the King of Mercia who ordered it constructed as a western delineation of his kingdom. Beyond the border, much of which is still visible today, the Welsh people continued their own Celtic culture and language, totally distinct from that of the Anglo-Saxons to the east. In the 9th Century, the Vikings (Norsemen) began their raids, as the names of some coastal towns and islands testify, such as Swansea, Great Orme, and Skomer, but apart from these few areas, they did not apparently settle in great numbers as they did in northern England.

In 855 A.D., Rhodri Mawr (*Rhodri the Great*) became King of Powys as well as much of the rest of Wales. Successful in warding off Danish attacks, he enjoyed a welcome period of unity and stability. Unfortunately for the future of an independent Wales, his death in 878 was followed by a period of internal strife. Rhodri was killed fighting an English army. It was left to his grandson, Hywel Dda (*Howell the Good*) to re-establish some sort of predominance among the various petty kingdoms of Wales that had re-emerged folllowing the death of Rhodri by keeping the peace with his English neighbors through conciliation.

In his reign, lasting from 904 to 950, Hywel's territories were known as Deheubarth, which united with Gwynedd and Powys to cover most of Wales with the exception of Glamorgan in the southeast. The only Welsh king to have earned the title "The Good," he is described in the great medieval history, The *Brut Y Tywysogion* (The Chronicle of the Princes) as "the chief and most praiseworthy of all the Britons."

During Hywel's reign at least, the major struggle was against outside influences, especially English attempts at control. It is for his brilliant codification of Welsh law, however, not for any military prowess, that the king is best remembered. It was the codification of the myriad of Welsh laws and customs into a single, unified system-*Cyfraith Hywel* (The Law of Hywel) has been seen as being far in advance of much English law. For one thing, it gave significant status to women, who were guaranteed certain rights that did not become part of the laws of England for over one thousand years. Most significant was the fact that the majority of the surviving documents are in Welsh, with only a few in Latin — another sign of the legitimacy of the language of the Cymry.

There was one great drawback. Welsh law specified that a father's lands be divided among all his sons, rather than be given intact to the eldest son. This led to unforeseen and tragic results for Wales. Many historians see it as a main reason for preventing the build up of a unified, powerful state such as occurred in neighboring England, in which there was a single heir.

In the development of the Welsh nation, which he seems to have kept free from the ravages of the marauding Vikings, Hywel's influence cannot be underestimated, yet even with all his statecraft, authority and fame, he could not succeed in creating a fully united, independent state that would endure his passing and withstand the coming of the rapacious Normans.

Almost immediately after his decisive victory over Harold and the Saxon army in 1066, William of Normandy set about establishing a strong, centralized kingdom in England. To help govern Wales, he set up powerful, semi-independent earldoms on the borders — at Hereford, Shrewsbury, and Chester. From these heavily fortified bases, military zones we call *the Marches*, the Norman "Marcher Lords" were able to completely colonize Gwent by 1087 and much of the rest of Southeast Wales as early as 1100.

Many princes of Wales resisted the Norman advances into their terrritories. In the year 1200, Llywelyn ap Iorwerth, the grandson of Owain Gwynedd (who had become pre-eminent in Wales during the latter half of the 12th Century) became ruler of the kingdom of Gwynedd, and under his strong and determined leadership, Wales was once more united as a single political unit. In 1205, Llywelyn married the English princess Joan, daughter of King John; and at a conference held at Aberdyfi in 1216, the Welsh leader was recognized as a legitimate Prince of Wales.

Llywelyn died in 1240. After his death, quarrels between his two sons Dafydd and Gruffudd undid practically all that their father had accomplished. In 1247, at the Treaty of Woodstock, East Gwynedd was ceded to King Henry. Then, in 1254, the English king showed his control by granting all the Crown lands in Wales to his young son, Prince Edward.

It was up to another Llywelyn, Llywelyn ap Gruffudd, the grandson of ap Iorwerth, to restore the situation. Through military conquest, after imprisoning his brothers and taking the kingdom of Gwynedd for himself, Llywelyn was able to re-unite much of his country in order to assert his claim to be called Prince of Wales, a title officially granted by Henry 111 at the Treaty of Montgomery (depicted: Prince Llywelyn).

At long last, it seemed that the ancient dream of the Welsh people had been realized — they had their own prince, they governed their own territories, under their own laws, and were able to conduct their own affairs in their own language relatively free from English influence. Wales was poised to take a place among the developing independent nation states of Europe. The accession to the English throne of Edward 1 in 1272 completely reversed the tide of affairs. The great struggle had to begin anew.

Disappointed by the acclaim given to his brother, and supported by Edward, Dafydd defected to the English. King Edward then took a huge army into Wales to punish the Welsh leader. Consequently, after suffering heavy defeats in the field and lacking any significant support, Llywelyn's great achievement at Montgomery was completely negated. At the Treaty of Aberconwy in 1277, he was forced to accept humiliating terms and to give up most of his recently acquired lands, keeping only Gwynedd west of the River Conwy.

Edward then followed up his successes by building English strongholds around the perimeter of what remained of Llywelyn's possessions. Strong, easily defended, forbidding castles were erected at the strategic points of Flint, Rhuddlan, Aberystwyth, and Builth, garrisoned by large detachments of English soldiers and their families, and settled by merchants and immigrants. The harsh methods used by Edward to control the conquered principality were soon to produce a major revolt.

An entry in *Brut y Tywysogion* reads: "The gentlefolk of Wales, despoiled of their liberty and their rights, came to Llywelyn ap Gruffudd and revealed to him with tears their grievous bondage to the English; and they made known to him that they preferred to be slain in war for their liberty than to suffer themselves to be unrighteously trampled upon by foreigners."

Edward had to devote the whole of his English kingdom's resources to deal with the "malicious, accursed" Welsh, yet it was a mere chance encounter that effectively ended the Welsh dream. Separated from the main body of his army, Llywelyn somehow got involved in a minor skirmish in which, unrecognized at first, he was killed by an English knight (depicted: Llywelyn's monument at Cilmeri, Powys).

After Llywelyn's death, the resistance of the Welsh people came to an inevitable end. Llywelyn's brother Dafydd was quickly captured and executed as a traitor. In 1294, the *Statute of Rhuddlan* created the counties of Anglesey, Caernarfon, and Merioneth, to be governed by the Justice of North Wales; Flint, to be placed under the Justice of Chester; and the counties of Carmarthen and Cardigan to be left under the Justice of South Wales. The Welsh counties did not elect representatives to Parliament; they remained outside the jurisdiction of the central courts of Westminster. From that time forward, Wales was to live under an alien political system, playing a subordinate role as an integral part of the kingdom of England. It was as if a nation or a people never existed.

In 1301 King Edward made Lord Edward his son (born at Caernarfon Castle), Prince of Wales and Count of Chester. Ever since that date, these titles have been automatically conferred upon the first-born son of the English monarch. Edward then began his second massive castle-building program to create such world-heritage sites of today as Caernarfon, Conwy, Harlech, and Beaumaris in addition to the not so well known (or not so well visited) earlier structures at Flint and Rhuddlan.

The struggle continued, but occasional rebellions were easily crushed. It was not the arrival of Owain Glyndwr (depicted) in the early 15th Century that any Welsh leader felt confident enough to challenge their English overlords.

Though ultimately defeated, Glyndwr revived dreams of Welsh nationalism that had never really died. The accession of the first of the Welsh Tudor monarchs to the throne in 1485, however, helped create a long-lasting bond between the two nations. In 1536 the Act of Union permanently joined Wales firmly to England and made the use of its native language illegal. The first Welsh M.P.'s went to the House of Commons in London in 1542. As a political entity, Wales ceased to exist for the next four hundred and fifty-five years. Hopes of regaining some measure of independence were not ignited until the 20th century.

A Welsh Home Rule Bill was first introduced into the House of Commons in 1914 but ignored by Parliament. The majority of Welsh people wanted equality and recognition, not self-government. Besides, all parts of Britain were united in the long, costly struggle against Germany. A new political party, Plaid Cymru, came into being in 1925 in a belated attempt to restore a sense of pride in being Welsh, but it took forty years to achieve respectability and a measure of firm support.

Following WW II, the dominant British Labour Party had no intention of recognizing any Welsh attempts at achieving nationhood. Thanks to the untiring work of such patriots as James Griffiths, however, a tiny advance took place in 1948 when the Council of Wales was formed, and in the same year the Minister for Welsh Affairs came into being. In 1955, Cardiff was officially recognized as the capital of Wales. This significant event marked a beginning of the road to a National Assembly. In 1964, in the Labour government of Harold Wilson, ex-coal miner M.P. for Ammanford, tireless James "Jim" Griffiths became the first Secretary of State for Wales.

Another real break through occurred in 1964 when Gwynfor Evans was elected to Parliament for Carmarthen as Member for Plaid Cymru, devoted to self-government. In 1968 Elystan Morgan, MP for Cardigan helped form a Royal Commission to investigate the topic of devolution for Wales and Scotland.

When Britain joined the European Community in 1972, hopes arose for an elected Assembly for Wales. Plaid gained two more seats in Parliament; the Royal Commission on the Constitution recommended sweeping administrative changes. In 1976 it presented the Scotland and Wales Bill. The majority of Welsh Labour M.P's from the highly anglicized industrial South remained solidly opposed to any form of devolution. On St. David's Day, March 1st 1979, the hopes for a Welsh Assembly went down to a resounding defeat. For the time being, at least, it seemed as if the issue of an elected Assembly was dead and buried. It wasn't.

By 1995, it was apparent that political intrigue, mistrust, and outright misrule marked the Westminster government. What is known as the system of Quangos (important decisions being made by non-elected government bodies) had the effect of catapulting Plaid Cymru into second place in the political parties in Wales. Perhaps even more significant was that the three parties in favor of devolution won 90 percent of the poll. In 1997, many of the factors that had led to the defeat of the 1979 referendum were still present in 1997, yet subtle changes had been taking place.

Two influential newspapers the *Liverpool Daily Post* (read mainly in North Wales), and the *Western Mail* (read mainly in the South) advocated a "yes" vote. Disgust with the way affairs were handled in Westminster meant that there would be hearty support for the proposed changes: Wales was to be in the vanguard of a constitutional reform package that would include a referendum for an elected body. in the later proposals, only a simple majority would be needed to pass the Referendum Bill, whereas in the former, a majority of the electorate itself had been required for passage.

The Labour Government issued plans to establish a directly elected Assembly responsible for policies and public services in Wales. The trade unions in Wales, blaming the negative results of 1979 vote on the fall of the Labour Government and the seizing of power by the Tories, urged their members to vote for the proposed Assembly.

The proposed Assembly seemed to offer some control and influence over decisions affecting lives and communities; it would help give a proper sense of identity to Wales and also create a proper sense of Welsh nationhood. By a tiny majority, the people of Wales approved a government referendum. The National Assembly for Wales (Cynulliad Cenedlaethol Cymru) finally came into being in 1997. For the first time, Wales was going to be allowed some control of the way it was to be governed.

The vote to approve an Assembly did not mean that Wales gained full independence from the United Kingdom, but nevertheless, a vital break through was achieved in the long, hard struggle that is the history of the people of Wales.

Chapter Three: The Survival of the Welsh Language

Many consider the greatest wonder of Wales to be its magnificent scenery, but for those who know and honor this lovely land, the biggest wonder of all must certainly be the survival of the Welsh language in the face of almost impossible odds. It certainly surprises many visitors to Wales to see road signs in a language that is one of the oldest in Europe and so remarkably different from English.

On the European continent, as a result of the administrative skills and military power of Rome, the majority of the Celtic languages eventually gave way to those stemming from Latin. Very few modern European languages are derived from *Celtic*, despite its former widespread use. But in mainland Britain, at least for a few hundred years after the Roman victories on mainland Europe, the Celts held on to much of their customs and especially to their distinctive language which has survived today as *Welsh* (depicted: Croeso i Gymru: Welcome to Wales)

This language, used throughout most of Britain at the time of the Roman invasions (except in the far north where Pictish survived for a while) was derived from a branch of Celtic known as *Brythonic*; it later gave rise to Welsh, Cornish and Breton. These differ from other Celtic languages derived from the branch known as *Goidelic*: namely, Irish, Scots, and Manx Gaelic (now confined to a western fringe in Ireland, to the north and west of Scotland, or to the history books as an extinct spoken tongue)

During the four hundred years of Roman occupation, the Celtic tongue survived in Britain as the medium of everyday speech, Latin being used mainly administrative purposes. Eventually, the majority language of Britain can be called *Romano-British*: a great deal of Latin words entered the native vocabulary, and many of these are still found in modern-day Welsh.

Today's visitors are surprised to find hundreds of place names containing the following: pont (bridge), sant (Saint), and mor (sea). Other Welsh words with Latin derivations are: ffenest (window), pysgod (fish), milltir (mile), mil (thousand), milwr (soldier), mêl (honey), melys (sweet), cyllell (knife), ceffyl (horse), perygl (danger), ceffyl (horse), eglwys (church), milwr (soldier), cantor (singer), llyfr (book), trist (sad) ysgrifennu (to write), pechadur (sinner), Iago (James), and many others (though many of these may have entered the language in subsequent centuries).

Sometime in the 7th Century A.D. during the time of the Germanic invasions of Britain, a Welsh Bishop heard a Saxon's voice on the bank of the River Severn and was filled with foreboding at the sound. The troubled bishop recorded his unsettling experience thus: "For the kinsman of yonder strange-tongued man whose voice I heard across the river...will obtain possession of this place, and it will be theirs, and they will hold it in ownership." The prediction came true in many parts of Wales. During the centuries of warfare with the Saxon invaders, the native Brythonic language gradually disappeared from much of lowland Britain. A sign of its demise is that very few words were adopted into the English language (surviving examples are coomb, coracle, eisteddfod, cromlech, avon, avalon and perhaps a few others).

The Anglo-Saxon invaders called the native peoples "brittas" and "brittisch," as well as "walas" or " wealas," the latter terms denoting foreigners or those who spoke the Celtic languages. The Welsh people called themselves *Cymry* as well as *Brythoniaid.* The Welsh word for their country is *Cymru* (Kumree), the land of the Comrades; the people are also known as *Cymry* and the language as *Cymraeg.*

When Edward 1st conquered Wales, its independence was finished. His statute of Rhuddlan (1284) set up English style counties and English style jurisdiction. This was only the beginning: from 1536 on, following the Act of Union, English was to be the only language of the courts of Wales, and those using the Welsh language were not to receive public office in the territories of the king. It now seemed that the Welsh language itself was doomed.

In 1547, William Salesbury came to the rescue. Alarmed at what he considered the baseness of the Welsh tongue, he wrote: "And take this advice from me; unless you save and correct and perfect the language before the extinction of the present generation, it will be too late afterwards." He took action to correct the situation by helping bring back the language to a respected position. He collaborated with Richard Davies, Bishop of St. David's, on a Welsh version of *The Book of Common Prayer* and *The New Testament*, both of which were published in 1567. In 1588, the masterful translation of the whole Bible itself, the climax of the whole movement, made Welsh the language of public worship and thus much more than a generally despised peasant tongue.

Completed by Bishop William Morgan with a group of fellow scholars, the *Welsh Bible* was revised in 1620 by Dr John Davies of Mallwyd and Richard Parry, Bishop of St Asaph. Most of the nearly one thousand copies of the earlier book had been lost or worn out. In 1630, the Welsh Bible, in a smaller version (*Y Beibl Bach*) was introduced into homes in Wales; and as the only book affordable to many families, it became the one book from which the majority of the people could learn to read and write.

In addition, poorer families, unable to afford the Bible, were able to share its contents in meetings held at the homes of neighbors or in their churches or chapels. Later on, countless generations of children were taught its contents in Sunday Schools. It is in this way, therefore, that the Welsh Bible "saved" the language from possible extinction. But the battle was far from won. In many areas it was being eroded rapidly.

In the last half of the 19th century, the great increase in industrialization of South Wales meant a flood of immigrants into the five valleys. Despite being expanded and strengthened by the Welsh-speaking newcomers, the Welsh community in the industrialized areas of the country began its inevitable decline. By the end of the century, it was ultimately unable to absorb the vast influx of non-Welsh speakers into its own language culture. The repercussions are felt strongly today as only one in five of the inhabitants of Wales use Welsh as an everyday language.

In Flintshire there had long been deliberate attempts to stamp out the Welsh language: a traveler to the area as early as 1799 described the situation thus: any child detected in speaking a Welsh word was immediately degraded with the "Welsh lump," a large piece of lead fastened to a string, and suspended round the neck of the offender. "The mark of ignominy had the desired effect: all the children of Flintshire speak English very well."

Such drastic measures were highly successful in many other areas. In 1804 John Evans wrote, "North Wales is becoming English." In the same year, describing another border county, Benjamin Heath Malkin wrote:

> *The language of Radnorshire is almost universally English. In learning to converse with their Saxon neighbours they have forgotten the use of their vernacular tongue.*

The Welsh language managed to hang on in other areas, only to incur increasing hostility.

In 1881, the Aberdare Commission's report showed that provisions for intermediate and higher education in Wales lagged behind those in the other parts of Britain; it suggested that there should be two new Welsh universities, Cardiff and Bangor. It was found, however, that there was a lack of adequately trained students for these new colleges and thus, in 1889 the *Welsh Intermediate Act* came into being. It gave the new county councils the power to raise a levy (to be matched by the Government) for the provision of secondary schools. In 1896 came the Central Welsh Board to oversee these schools.

The result was that thousands of Welsh children from all levels of society were able to continue their education at a secondary level. Another result, however, was the continued decline of the status accorded the Welsh language, for the new secondary schools were thoroughly English, only very few even bothering to offer Welsh lessons. An educated class of Welsh people was thus created that fostered the cultural traditions of their country in the language of England.

In the middle years of the 20th century, the great increase in the number of people owning automobiles and the improvements in the road system meant that many areas in Wales were easily reached from many English towns and cities. Welsh communities found themselves inundated with flood of new residents or casual visitors who were either too disinterested in learning the Welsh language or were too old and who just couldn't be bothered.

It was far too easy to get by perfectly well in Wales without knowing a single word of its language. The North Wales coast, known as "the Welsh Riviera," became first a weekend playground, and then an extension of, Merseyside, with all the problems of that conurbation. Similarly, mid-Wales was transformed by a huge influx from the Midlands. Birmingham accents became common, even in such centres of Welsh culture as Aberystwyth and Machynlleth

From almost one million speakers of the language in 1931, the number fell to just over 500,000 in less than fifty years, despite the large increase in the population. Strongholds of the old language and its attendant culture were crumbling fast, and it seemed that nothing could be done to stem the tide. Then something of a minor miracle occurred.

In Pontarddulais in 1962, at the Summer School held by Plaid Cymru, the seeds of a new movement were planted. Mainly involving a younger, active post-War Welsh generation, many of them college students, a new society, Cymdeithas yr Iaith Gymraeg (Society for the Welsh language) decided to take matters in hand. The decline of the language had to be halted and the Government's hand had to be forced.

Saviors to many, scoundrels and troublemakers to others, the frustrated members of the newly formed society were galvanized into action after a talk given on the radio by Saunders Lewis in February 1962. In his address on the BBC entitled *Tynged yr Iaith* (Fate of the Language), Lewis asked his listeners to make it impossible for local or central government business to be conducted in Wales without the use of the Welsh language. This was the only way to ensure its survival. Plaid Cymru could not help, he reasoned; it was too much a political party. Who was to take up the banner?

The answer came quickly. During the same year, a Cymdeithas activist decided to ignore an English language summons to appear in court for allowing his girl friend to ride sidesaddle on his bicycle. The protests began. At Trefechan Bridge, at a busy intersection in Aberystwyth that controlled the access and egress from the town center, dozens of the society sat down in the road to stop all traffic from coming in or going out. They sat all day to defy the local authorities (and irate local drivers) to remove them. Many were dragged off to face prison sentences.

This was the beginning of a series of protests and civil disobedience that was to last for the next twenty years. Undeterred by their forcible removal, arrests, and prison sentences for disturbing the peace, and led by such activists as Fred Fransis and folk-singer Dafydd Iwan (depicted), the society began a serious campaign. Cymdeithas pressed for the right to use Welsh on all government documents, from Post Office forms to television licenses, from driving permits to income tax forms. In particular, the society engaged in surreptitious nighttime activities, removing English language only signposts and directional aids, or obliterating them with green paint.

The activists were inspired by a Dafydd Iwan ballad, "Painting the World Green, Boys." All over Wales, early morning motorists were faced with the green paint daubed slogan that had mysteriously appeared overnight, or with the equally mysteriously missing road sign.

It became increasingly frustrating and expensive for local authorities and the Ministry of Transport to remove, renovate or replace damaged signs. Eventually, in 1963, faced with an ever-growing campaign, increased police and court costs, destruction of government property, and the vociferous demands for action, the central Government decided to establish a committee to examine the legal status of Welsh.

The report, issued two years later, recommended that the Welsh language be given equal validity with English, a diluted version of which was placed into the Welsh Language Act of 1967. It made special reference to the use of Welsh in legal proceedings and on official forms.

The *Gittins Report* recommended that every child in Wales be given the opportunity to become reasonably bilingual by the end of the primary stage, a recommendation that was put into effect in the 1990's.

There was a new feeling in the land of Wales. The young were answering the call of Saunders Lewis and others to keep their language and culture alive. The older generation began to reconsider their indifference or their passiveness in letting the language die. Dafydd Iwan and his contemporaries inaugurated a whole new movement in Welsh music (dominated as it was by the old Methodist traditions), translating popular English and American songs into Welsh, or writing stirring new lyrics and music of protest. The popularity of traditional hymns sung by male voice choirs found a competitor – the loud, cheerful rhythms of the new folk rock bands.

Groups such as *Ar Log* rediscovered and popularized old folk tunes and brought them up to date. Even the revered, staid (and often-pompous) eisteddfod entered into the spirit, each year erecting a Roc Pavilion where such groups could attract the young who had previously been sorely neglected. Many Welsh Rock groups have become internationally known. Great progress also took place in the schooling of young children.

The ripple affect spread throughout Wales, especially its primary schools. Llanelli Welsh School had opened its doors as early as 1947 to teach primary children through the medium of the Welsh language. The idea slowly but eventually caught on in other areas. The radical happenings of the 1960's led to the reintroduction of the Welsh language in other schools. It was warmly welcomed by many of the townsfolk, and a new generation of children who can read and speak and write Welsh may help ensure the future of first, Plaid Cymru, and ultimately, of the nation itself

In 1971, as a response to heavy demands, the Welsh Nursery School Movement (Sefydlu Mudiad Ysgolion Meithrin) was formed. In many totally English-speaking areas, parents sent their children to such nursery schools, and enrolled themselves in evening classes to learn the necessary phrases to continue the use of

Welsh at home. The broadcast media also belatedly helped revive the language. The BBC had begun broadcasting to Welsh listeners in 1922, but its programs were in English. Beginning in 1927, Radio Eireann, the voice of the Irish Republic, broadcast the only regular Welsh language material.

The head of the first BBC station in Cardiff ignored the protests of those who wished to hear Welsh language programs. At the time there were a million speakers of Welsh, but many believed that their own language was inferior. A propitious decline was about to begin. Perhaps the Welsh language would have even advanced in status and numbers had it been given sufficient air time in the 1920's and 30's. One problem was that most Welsh listeners enjoyed radio's English language programs. Their enjoyment came at the expense of their cherished native tongue.

A dedicated few, however, continued their protests. Eventually, reluctantly, the BBC studio at Bangor, in North Wales, began broadcasting Welsh language programs in 1935, and in July of 1937 the Welsh Region of the BBC finally began to broadcast on a separate wavelength. In 1962, BBC Wales produced only six hours a week of Welsh language television programs. Among many others, Hadyn Williams, Director of Education in Flintshire (responsible for setting up two Welsh secondary schools in that county), wasn't satisfied. He established a company to broadcast to areas out of reach of the English transmitters. Demands soon arose for a separate channel for all-Welsh programs. Ironically, many English speakers were in full support as they resented the Welsh language broadcasts on what they considered their channels.

When the Government refused to honor its commitment to the proposed channel, a vigorous protest movement developed, with thousands of Plaid Cymru members vowing to refuse to pay their television license fees (and their subsequent fines) and prepared to be imprisoned. Gwynfor Evans (depicted), the highly respected leader of Plaid Cymru, announced that he would undergo a hunger strike to the death, and the Government capitulated.

On 2 November 1982, the people of Wales finally got their Welsh-language channel, "S4C" (Sianel Pedwar C). The spin off was immense.

In Cardiff, where most of the programs originated, a new urban class was created in which it became fashionable to speak Welsh. For the first time, film directors, translators, language dubbers, editors, writers and so on all were able to work together through the medium of the ancient tongue. The Channel produced not only some very highly regarded television programs, but also turned out films equal to those of Hollywood and London.

In early 2010, a proposed new law on the Welsh language was published by the Assembly. The Welsh Language Measure would lead to rights for Welsh speakers to receive services in the language. Firms in areas such as telecoms, gas and electricity would face sanctions including fines if they fail to meet language service delivery standards. As well as public sector bodies, it will bind certain specified organisations in the private sector to provide services in Welsh, including gas, water and electricity suppliers, bus and railway services, sewerage services and telecommunications.

A language commissioner would replace the Welsh Language Board and work to promote and facilitate the use of Welsh and equality between Welsh and English. The measure would also confirm official status for the Welsh language,

Heritage Minister, Alun Ffred Jones said the measure "...will answer the call for Welsh speakers to have the right to receive services in Welsh - and will establish a Welsh Language Commissioner to enforce these rights."

Plaid Cymru leader Ieuan Wyn Jones said history would show the measure to be a "significant milestone" in the history of the language, making a real difference to those who wish to use the language in their every-day lives and access services through the medium of Welsh. He said: "Those people will have rights for the first time in our history, and that can only lead to greater equality, and a nation that is ever-more comfortable with its two languages."

Perhaps most important is the subtle change in attitude towards the language brought about by the tangible advantages that can be gained by its speakers in all fields, not just the social and academic. Welsh-language activists want to make sure that it would be worth while for everyone living in Wales to learn Welsh—that the learning of the language be given priority as an important labor, of equal merit with anything else in one's life.

Chapter Four: The Red Dragon (Y Ddraig Goch)

The standard of Wales is a red dragon on a green and white background. It is not represented on the national Union flag of Britain, which consists of the red upright cross of St. George of England on a white background; the white diagonal cross of St. Andrew of Scotland on a blue background; and the red diagonal cross of St. Patrick of Ireland on a white background (the term "Union Jack" more properly refers to the ensign flown by the Royal Navy).

The cross of St. Andrew was added to the Cross of St. George in 1707 when Scotland joined the Union. The Union flag that was flown in the American Colonies before the Revolution does not include the cross of St. Patrick. This was added in 1800, when Ireland became part of Great Britain and remained until 1921, when the island nation was divided into the Free State (that later became the Irish Republic of Eire) and Ulster (or Northern Ireland).

The Red Dragon of Wales (*Y Ddraig Goch*) goes back a very long time, long before the Union flag was ever put together. As a national symbol for Wales, it predates its adaptation by the Tudors, for it is perhaps the very first mythical beast in British heraldry. Legend has Magnus Maximus (Macsen Wledig) and his Romano-British soldiers carrying the red dragon ("Draco") to Rome on their banners in the fourth century.

The dragon was adopted in the early fifth century by the Welsh kings of Aberffraw to symbolize their authority after the Roman withdrawal from Britain. By the seventh century, it was known as the Red Dragon of Cadwallader, forever after to be associated with the people of Wales. The 9th century historian Nennius mentions the red dragon, and it was also referred to by Geoffrey of Monmouth in his *Historia Regum Britanniae* (1120-1129).

In Geoffrey's account, Uther Pendragon was the father of Arthur; his name translates as "Dragon Head." Uther had a dream of a dragon appearing in a comet. When he became king, he had two dragon standards made. It was Geoffrey of Monmouth who told the tale of two dragons fighting, the red and the white, representing the Welsh and the English respectively. In the story, the red dragon is overthrown by the white, signifying English control of the lands of Britain.

The red dragon banner, however, continued to fly proudly; it was used by the Normans in Britain and apparently was used as the British standard at the Battle of Crecy (1346), in which Welsh archers, dressed in their beloved green and white, played so prominent a part. It may have been during this battle that the tradition of the wearing of the leek first began.

Though Owain Glyndwr had raised his dragon standard in 1400 as a symbol of revolt against the English Crown, the dragon continued to be used by the Tudor monarchs. It signified their direct descent from one of the noble families of Wales. At Holywell, in Flintshire, there is a dragon carved over one of the arches beside St. Winifred's Well in honor of Henry V11, the first Tudor king, who displayed the red dragon of Cadwallader, from whom he claimed descent, on the Tudor colours of white and green. Until this time it was probably golden. Henry's standard was white over green "with the red dragon over all." His eldest son, the Prince of Wales was to be the new king Arthur, uniting the whole of Britain, but he died before he could be crowned.

The dragon reappeared briefly as a supporter of the arms of the Commonwealth under Cromwell. During Henry VIII's reign the red dragon on a green and white background became a favorite emblem on many of the Royal Navy ships; it was also a particular favorite of the Tudor Queen Elizabeth I, "that red-headed Welsh harridan," as she has been called by historian A. L. Rowse. The dragon was replaced by a unicorn on the orders of King James I (who was also James VI of Scotland). It did not reappear on the Royal Badge of Wales until 1807.

On March 11th, 1953, it was announced that Her Majesty Queen Elizabeth 11 had approved that 'the existing red dragon badge, which was appointed as a Royal Badge for Wales over one-hundred-and-fifty years ago, should be honourably augmented by enclosing it in a scroll carrying the words in green lettering on a white background and surmounting it a Royal Crown." The new badge contained the old Welsh motto: *Y Ddraig Goch Ddyry Cychwyn* (The Red Dragon Inspires action).

A new Royal Badge of Wales based on the arms of Llywelyn ap Gruffudd was approved in May 2008. St. Edward's Crown sits atop a continuous scroll, which, together with a wreath consisting of the plant emblems of the four countries of the United Kingdom, surrounds the shield. The motto, *Pleidiol wyf i'm Gwlad* (*I am true to my country*), from the National Anthem of Wales is also found on Welsh design £1 coins. The new badge appears on the cover of Assembly Measures passed by the National Assembly for Wales.

The present national flag of Wales (the red dragon on a green and white background), seems to have come into prominence only in the early part of the 20th century, being used at the 1911 Caernarfon Investiture of Edward, the Prince of Wales. It wasn't officially recognized as the national flag of the principality until 1959 when Queen Elizabeth was successfully petitioned for its national use by the Gorsedd.

Controversy over the correct version of the flag was settled that year when a statement from the Minister of State for Wales announced that "...only the Red Dragon on a green and white flag...shall be flown on Government buildings in Wales, and, where appropriate, in London."

The Red Dragon flies proudly over public and private buildings all over Wales, and appears on all the "Welcome to Wales" (Croeso i Gymru) signs at the various border crossings. It has endeared itself to the Welsh people as a symbol of pride in their history and their hopes for their future.

Chapter Five: Welsh Christianity

About three thousand years ago, the Celtic peoples brought their languages and their pagan religion to Britain. From what we know of the druids, their leaders of religion and guardians of tradition, they did not commit their learning to writing. In 44 A.D. Emperor Claudius sent an expedition to subdue the grain-rich southeastern territories of Britain. It was not long before the victorious Roman armies arrrved in North Wales.

Roman historian Tacitus described the druids assembled along the shores of the Menai Strait (in present-day Anglesey) as being "ranged in order, with their hands uplifted, invoking the gods and pouring forth horrible imprecations." By attacking and killing these druids, their wives and children, the Romans were able to defeat the brave but ragged formations drawn up against them.

Thanks to the missionary work of Martin of Tours in Gaul and the edict of 400 A.D. that made Christianity the only official worship of the Empire, the new religion was brought to Britain, where it was quickly adopted by the romanized Britons, replacing their adoration of Mithras. The old Celtic gods had to slink off into the mountains and hills to hide, reappearing fitfully and almost apologetically only in the poetry and myths of later ages.

When Rome fell in the fifth century, the Christian Church survived in Wales, mostly in a monastic form. In Southeast Wales, centers of Christianity flourished under such figures as Saints Dyfrig, Illtud, and David. A monastic community was founded at Bangor, in the northwest, by Saint Deiniol in 525; and at Llanelwy in the Northeast by St Kentigern, who was succeeded as Bishop by Asaph in 570.

St. David's in Pembrokeshire is said to date from around the same time when David moved his monastery from Whitesand Bay to Glyn Rhosyn. Another great center of learning was established at Llanilltyd Fawr by Saint Illtyd in the 6th century that also trained missionaries for Ireland. From there, under such outstanding leaders as Columba and Aidan, the English were eventually won over to Christianity.

Welsh churchmen such as David, Padarn, Teilo and Deiniol were recognized throughout the land for their piety and learning.

(Depicted: St. Brynach's Cross) What little we do know concerning David comes from the late 11th Century *The Life of St. David* by Rhigfarch (Ricemarch) but supplemented by Geraldus Cambrensis around 1200. David's fame as a missionary reached Ireland and Brittany, and from the 12th Century the church named for him at St. David's became an important place of pilgrimage. Although David died in 589, Wales did not adopt him as its patron saint until the 18th Century, with the reputed date of his death (March lst) chosen as the day of a national festival. In 597, Augustine was sent by Pope Gregory to convert the Saxons of England, establishing his seat at Canterbury and given authority over most of the English kingdoms by King Egbert The Church in Wales remained aloof, keeping its own system of organization and customs. It did not conform to the new forms of the Roman Church made permanent by the Synod of Whitby in 664.

As late as 731, the English churchman and historian Bede wrote, "The Britons for the most part have a natural hatred for the English and uphold their own bad customs against the true Easter of the Catholic Church." Yet, by the year 768, the Welsh Church seems to have fully adopted the new system.

After the Norman Conquest of Britain in the llth century, additional cathedrals were built in Wales at Llandaff, near Cardiff; at Glyn Rhosyn (St. David's) in Pembrokeshire; and Brecon (formerly the Benedictine Priory of St. John). St. Woolos in Newport became a cathedral only in 1949, but a church was built on the site in the 5th century by Lord Gwynllyw.

During the reign of the Tudors, Britain's conversion to Protestantism was relatively peaceful compared to what transpired on the Continent. The majority of people in Wales were closely allied to their fellow islanders under threats of invasion from Spain and the fear of a return to what was considered a morally and spiritually bankrupt foreign church (or foreign rule, in the case of Mary Tudor and Philip of

Spain). In spite of the activities of a few important Catholic intellectuals, mostly in exile on the Continent, the coercive power of the state kept Wales in the Protestant fold.

The situation had been helped immeasurably by the fortuitous arrival of and widespread dissemination of the Welsh Bible. In 1546, Sir John Price of Brecon published the first book in the Welsh language, his collection of basic religious texts *Yn Llyvyr Hwnn* (In This Book). Tradition has it that the very first book actually printed in Wales itself was *Y Drych Gristianogawl* (The Christian Mirror), produced in a cave at Llandudno, as a surreptitious counter-reformation text in 1585.

The pioneer of publishing in Welsh, however, was not John Price, but William Salesbury, whose scholarship was astonishing. He published books in English as well as Welsh, covering linguistics, proverbs, science, law, and of course, religion. In 1547 he wrote, "If you do not wish utterly to depart from the faith of Christ...obtain the holy scripture in your own tongue as your happy ancestors, the ancient British, had it."

After the 1553 English Prayer book had abandoned the belief in transubstantiation, thus, according to Professor John Davies, "establishing Protestantism in the territories of the crown of England," Salesbury worked tirelessly to make the scriptures known to the Welsh people in their own language. He had begun this task with his Welsh-English dictionary of 1547 and in 1551 he published his *Kynniver Llyth a Ban*, a translation of the main texts of the Prayer Book.

In 1563, after John Penry and others had petitioned Queen and Parliament, a bill was passed ordering that the Bible be translated into Welsh. Penry was helped by the fact that Elizabeth and her parliament were appalled at the slow progress in of the Welsh people in learning the English language, and perhaps at their sluggishness in converting from Catholicism.

The Government welcomed Penry's suggestions, thinking that by having Welsh translations placed next to the English texts in Church, the congregations would learn English. It was also a good method to establish Protestantism in Wales, certainly the main reason. The Welsh bishops entrusted the momentous task mainly to Salesbury, who had prepared the way with his earlier translation of the Prayer Book.

The work was completed by Bishop Morgan, then a Parish priest, whose scholarship was unmatched; he had studied Hebrew, Greek and Latin at Cambridge. In 1588 with a group of fellow-scholars, including the brilliant Richard Davies, he completed his work. Morgan's expectations, like Salesbury's before him, were mainly to present God's word to his people in their own language and thus save them from damnation. Its influence upon the subsequent religious direction of the Welsh people was totally unexpected; it had enormous effects upon both their language and their literature.

In 1620, Dr John Davies of Mallwyd was responsible for minor corrections and standardization in his revision version that is a classic of Welsh literature, similar to the King James Bible in English. Of his Bible, Dr. Davies wrote:

> *It is impossible to believe that God would have seen fit to keep this language alive until these days, after so many crises in the history of the nation...had He not intended His name to be called and His great works to be proclaimed in it.*

Most scholars agree that the influence of the Welsh Bible is incalculable: because of it, and strengthened by it, through their faith, their religious leaders, their language and their literature, the people of Wales were able to continue their struggle. On the other hand, though many of their great families and scholars had remained Catholic far longer than many of their counterparts in England, the great majority of Welsh people were generally apathetic to any organized forms of religion apathy. They had their precious Bible; it was enough.

After the execution of Charles in 1649, Parliament was anxious to provide sufficient ministers of the gospel to reach those areas of the country they deemed sufficiently in need, Wales being perhaps on top of their list. In 1650 was passed the *Act for the Better Propagation and Preaching of the Gospel* that appointed many prominent government officials as Commissioners in Wales.

Their task was to investigate complaints against the resident clergy (who had mostly supported Charles), following the doctrine of Divine Right (now anathema to the Puritans). They were also given authority to eject those ministers they considered unsuitable or disloyal, and to appoint "godly and painful men" to replace those deprived of their livings.

Once again, however, it seems that Welsh congregations seemed to take most of the changes in their stride. Puritan doctrines had long been taking root in many of the urban centers and market towns, aided and abetted by wealthy London merchants. Since having their own Bible in 1588, in any case (as Elizabeth had wished) the Welsh were fast becoming a "people of the Book." The traveling clergymen could appeal to those who already had a sense of religious independence; furthermore, they were able to preach to them in their own language. They were thus welcomed in communities all over Wales.

A huge influence came from the zeal of evangelists such as William Wroth, Walter Cradock, and Vavasor Powell. The latter, who first advocated public hymn singing, was the most dynamic preacher and recruiter of them all. From the efforts of such tireless and inspired workers came the founding of the first "gathered church" of independents in Wales in 1639.

In 1649 the first Baptist Church in Wales was founded at Ilston in the Gower Peninsula, near Swansea by John Miles. The seeds were thus planted for a new religious consciousness in Wales that had an enormous impact on the future political, social and cultural development of the nation. *The Propagation Act*, in addition to rooting out dissident clergymen, attempted to establish in Britain a national system of schools. In Wales, sixty-three new schools were opened in the larger towns. In them,

Children of both sexes were taught to read, write and count (and memorize the scriptures) free of charge. Though the Commission was not renewed in 1653, "suitable" ministers continued to be selected by the agents of Parliament, and many gifted and enthusiastic preachers arrived in Wales to live and work.

The influence of such tireless spiritual leaders was a lasting one, and the nonconformist chapels that sprang up everywhere in their wake, such as those of the Independents, Baptists, Quakers and others created a heritage that until very recently was still regarded as an integral part of the Welsh character. It certainly left a fertile field to be tilled by the Methodists in the next century.

In the meantime, for those in power in Westminster, more rigid control of the Welsh was needed: the forces of Nonconformity were moving too rapidly for the likes of King and Parliament, a little frightened of the democratization of the church. Consequently, congregations in England and Wales had to be brought back into line: the *Act of Uniformity* of 1662 required all ministers to assent to the rites and liturgy of the Established Church, restored with the accession of Charles 11 two years earlier.

Next came T*he Clarendon Code* (four acts passed 1661-65) that imposed severe penalties on those who refused to conform to the Act of Uniformity. For many, it was far too late. They were determined not to return to the fold and sought other lands in which to practice their faith. The result was that whole congregations moved from Wales to the New World where they became instrumental in setting up such settlements as that of the Welsh Quakers that later became the Commonwealth of Pennsylvania. (In the little village of Llangaches in Monmouthshire, the Mother Church of Welsh nonconformity was modeled after those established by the Puritans in the American colonies).

An even more severe burden for the religious independents came with the first *Conventicle Act* in 1664 that prohibited groups of more than five persons from assembling for religious worship other than that prescribed by the Church. Other Acts ensured that such sects as the Quakers and Baptists were forced to meet in secret or join their brethren over the Atlantic Ocean.

Even the *Toleration Act* of 1689 that allowed Dissenters to worship in their own chapels did nothing to keep them from being excluded from municipal government and the universities. It is noticeable that in the

American colonies, Welsh people quickly became prominent in both fields (Maryland colony had passed its own Toleration Act in 1649).

Among the people of Wales, Puritan writers continued their work with or without royal blessings. One of the most influential was Charles Edwards, who believed sincerely that the Welsh were God's chosen people, having replaced the fallen children of Israel or having been directly descended from "the Lost Tribes" themselves (a myth that remained widely popular in Wales for generations). Edwards's *Y Ffydd Ddi-ffuant* (The Sincere Faith, 1667) was an attempt to prove his claim. The widely read book deals with the history of the Christian religion, the moral history of the Welsh people themselves, and the spiritual condition of individual Welshman.

Religion was also the prime subject of many popular poets, of whom the most popular and influential was Rhys Prichard, Vicar of Llandovery, whose verses were published in 1681 as *Canwyll y Cymry* (the Candle of the Welsh). They were recited and learned by generation after generation of Welsh children

The 18th Century in Wales can be called "the Century of Methodism," for the lives of its people were altered immeasurably, for better or for worse, by the coming of the Spirit. Historians generally agree that it was as if a different Wales came to be invented out of the turmoil brought on by the benign neglect of the English Parliament, the Royal family, and the Welsh landed gentry. Wales needed new and effective leadership if it were to remain in any sense a nation, and this was provided, not by those in government at Westminster, nor by its great families, mostly gone over to the English cause, but by the soldiers of the Methodist Church.

When the great Methodist preachers burst upon the Welsh scene, they found the ground had been well prepared. We have already seen the results of the Propagation Act and of the pioneer Puritan laborers. Their work had been made relatively easy by the dismal state of the regular clergy in Wales.

One problem for the Church had been that the Parish priests no longer could receive their lucrative tithes, which had been awarded to the local gentry. The result was a dismal compensation for the clergy, few of whom had been to the university and very few of whom knew the language of their parishioners.

From 1713, not a single Welsh speaker was appointed to a Welsh bishopric for over 150 years. Appointments in Wales were seen as mere stepping stones for more lucrative positions east of Offa's Dyke: they were mostly filled by non-Resident clergy. The Established Church in Wales had neither the financial resources nor the willingness to reform itself; thus the way was open for the ministers of the new faith (depicted: Llandaff Cathdral). Before the Nonconformist movement could develop fully, however, and especially that part dominated by the Methodists, there had to be a groundwork laid in the field of general education among the masses, mostly ignorant and all too often ignored by those in authority. Hand in hand with the religious reformers, then, there was a burst of activity in more secular matters, such as teaching the people to read and write.

The new preaching zeal, with its emphasis on individual salvation, and especially by its emphasis on "the word," brought home the need for literacy and education and thus the demand for more printed works. The number of books printed in Welsh increased rapidly in the fifty years after the restoration of the Monarchy in 1660. As often in Welsh history, the impetus came from outside. In 1674, a charitable organization, the Welsh Trust, was set up in London by Thomas Gouge to establish English schools in Wales and to publish books in Welsh.

There were impressive results: over 500 books came off the printing presses set up in Wales in 1718 and 1721. Many of these were translations of popular English works, mainly Protestant tracts that encouraged private worship and prayers. Along with the six major editions of the Bible that appeared during the same period, they had the unpredicted effect of ensuring the survival of the Welsh language in an age where more than one scholar was predicting its rapid demise.

Of equal importance were the cheap catechisms and prayer books, highly prized by rural families who read them in family groups during the long, dark winter nights. One English writer in 1721 commented:

> *There is, I believe, no part of the nation [Britain] more inclined to be religious, and to be delighted with it, than the poor inhabitants of these mountains.*

So successful were educators, benefactors and itinerant teachers that it has been estimated that perhaps as many as one third or more of the population of Wales could read their scriptures by the time of churchman Griffith Jones' death in 1761. Jones had been greatly aided by such men as Stephen Hughes, who published religious literature in Welsh; wealthy landowner and patron Mrs. Bridget Bevan of Laugharne; and Sir John Philipps of Picton, one of the founders of the Society for the Promotion of Christian Knowledge begun in 1698 by Thomas Bray in England.

The three philanthropists had started a large number of charity schools in 1699. In these schools, set up all over Wales, in an attempt to deal with the widespread problems of poverty and ignorance, the Society allowed the use of Welsh alongside that of English and set up libraries in many of the towns. Jones, who had married John Philipps' sister, had realized that preaching alone was insufficient to ensure his people's salvation: they needed to read the scriptures for themselves. And to do this, of course, they had to be taught to read. In 1740 Jones wrote:

> *What length of time...how many hundreds of years must be allowed for the general attainment of English, and the dying away of the Welsh language: ... And in the mean time, while this is adoing...what myriads of poor ignorant souls must launch forth into the dreadful abyss of eternity, and perish for want of knowledge.*

Consequently, Jones persuaded the Society to donate Welsh Bibles from which he could teach people to read. As there were not enough qualified teachers in each parish to maintain a school, itinerant ministers were employed, and by this method, schools were conducted in almost every parish in Wales. Evening classes were set up for the laborers and farm workers and those who worked in the trades, and the "circulating schools" as they were called, have been regarded as one of the few great success stories in the history of Wales.

Eighteenth century Wales was thus made one of the most literate countries in Europe, with much of its population acquainted with the literary language of the Bible. Jones provided details each year of the number of pupils attending the circulating schools that showed almost half the total population of Wales was affected. Jones was the Rector of Llanddowror Parish and therefore not a Nonconformist minister; neverthless, his writings created a substantial Welsh reading public primed and ready to receive the appeal of the Methodists. The ability in such preachers as Hywel Harris was matched by their eloquence in the pulpit, and who obviously filled a great need among the masses.

Harris is known as the "Father of the Methodist Revival in Wales." Refused ordination by his Bishop at Oxford University because of his preaching activities, he was converted to the Methodist cause in 1735. He worked closely with other religious enthusiasts such as Daniel Rowland; William Williams; Peter Williams, who produced a very popular version of the Bible; and John Wesley, the English evangelist.

Another influential convert was Thomas Charles in 1784, who set up the successful Sunday School movement in North Wales that had such a profound and lasting influence on the language and culture of that region. Under his leadership, the British and Foreign Bible Society published the standardized text of their first Welsh Bible, and the Society for the Propagation of Christian Knowledge published an edition of the New Testament. Charles's own publication of the Welsh Bible in 1814, the year of his death, was also a major achievement.

The leadership of the Methodist Revival in Wales was shared by Daniel Rowland, who had converted in 1737. His sermons at his chapel at Llangeitho that made him famous were published in two volumes along with a number of other works in Welsh. Rowland's enthusiasm, along with that of his colleagues, attracted thousands of converts. Though their initial intention was to work within the Established Church, opposition from their Bishops, all of whom had little real interest in Wales and knew practically nothing of its language and culture, led finally to the schism of 1811 when an independent union was founded. This was the Calvinistic Methodist Church that is today known as the Presbyterian Church of Wales.

Some members of the so-called upper classes — the landed gentry — clung to the established Anglican Church; just about everyone else joined the new religion (picture: St David's Cathedral). The new movement provided the excitement and fervor that the established church had been lacking for so long. It certainly did much to pave the way for the rapid growth of the other non-conformist sects such as the Baptists and Independents. In addition, Methodism was responsible for producing two names that are outstanding in the cultural history of Wales, William Williams and Ann Griffiths.

Williams became a preacher and organizer of Methodist societies, but he is best remembered as the most important hymn writer that Wales has ever produced. His best-known hymn is one that has remained a standard, sung throughout Wales (even at rugby football games): *Cwm Rhondda*, sung to the words "Guide me, oh, thou great Jehovah."

Other great hymn writers of the period included David Charles, whose brother Thomas founded the Welsh Sunday School movement. David wrote many fine hymns, including *Llef* (A Cry) with its opening lines: "O Iesu Mawr, rho d'anian bur," and the equally classic funeral hymn *Crug y Bar*; and Evan Evans, who won many eisteddfod prizes for his poems and hymns.

Of all his contemporaries, however, some of them masters of their craft, only one was able to match William Williams in the sheer intensity and power of their writing, and that was Ann Griffiths. From

Dolwar Fach, a little village in Montgomeryshire, which subsequently became a centre of Methodist preaching, her intense spiritual and sensuous hymns show her abilities as a poet using rhythmic, melodious language that expresses so well her religious intensity and devotion to Jesus, her personal saviour and object of an almost obsessive love.

Though it is not her most well-known hymn, Ann's *Rhyfedd* was regarded by modern Welsh poet Saunders Lewis as "one of the greatest religious poems in any European language." Perhaps the most famous of Ann's hymns, however, and the one most often sung today, to the tune *Cwm Rhondda,* is "Wele'n sefyll rhwng y myrtwydd" (See him standing between the myrtles).

The earnestness of the new religion, out of which sprang such as William Williams and Ann Griffiths, greatly shaped the Welsh character for the next two centuries (the same kind of development took place in Scotland, where severe Calvinism replaced a native Celtic joy in life). Sin and evil were emphasized at the expense of delight in a natural spontaneity and love of life in all its forms.

The Methodist hymns, powerful and majestic became practically the only form of music known to much of the population of Wales. Traditional forms of music, folk dancing and long-practiced games and customs went by the wayside, many forever, unless preserved by a few gypsy families such as that of Abram Wood (*Teulu Abram Wood*) in North Wales.

The chapel became the main focal point of so much social life in Wales, creating an atmosphere that lasted right up until the end of World War II (depicted is Capel yr Annibynwyr, Fforestfach, Swansea). Yet all was not entirely melancholic; there were some remarkable individuals and some striking events that, in many ways, acted as a counterbalance to the religious atmosphere created by the Methodist Revival. And to be fair, it was Methodism that greatly aided the people of Wales in their ever-lasting struggle to retain their spirituality, their language and their sense of independence.

In 1904, an event began that helped shape the character of modern Wales. Starting in Cardiganshire and quickly spreading throughout Wales the "Great Revival" under the leadership of Evan Roberts and others. Helping to boost the Temperance Movement and the campaign for Church disestablishment., it swept many thousands along in a fervent spirit. In some areas, the revival meant the closure of many social clubs, the further loss of many of the old, secular folk songs, and led to that emphasis on public hymn-singing begun in the earlier Methodist Movement that has so often characterized groups of Welsh men and women ever since.

World War I brought the entire national revival of Wales to an end. Welsh manpower losses in the armed services were incalculable; they were never replaced as whole communities suffered greatly. The resulting disillusionment in the efficacy of religion to relieve suffering caused a rapid decline in chapel membership.

The status of the Anglican Church in Wales as the State Church was also in serious trouble. The largest denomination in Wales by virtue of its long history and traditions, its leaders were often out of touch with their parishioners. Before 1920, not a single bishop able to speak Welsh had been appointed to a Welsh see. Michael D. Jones's college at Bala was the only one in Wales that honoured the use of Welsh. At St. David's Theological College in Lampeter, a training school for Welsh clergy, there was no requirement to be able to read, speak, or write one single line in the language of their parishioners. Future clergymen studying at the college ridiculed the idea of learning any of the Welsh language.

In 1920, the Anglican Church was disestablished. By that time there was not too much interest in the matter. The worries of the economy, with the onset of the Depression were far more important matters to worry about. The workingman's club and the pub were now dominating life in the cities, the towns, and the Valleys. It has been that way ever since, except to add that television and the theme pub seem to have permanently replaced the chapel service in so many communities.

Chapter Six: Welsh Traditions

Though many Welsh traditions have been lost by the present generation, a great decline having set in during the dark days of World War 11, there are many that remain. Some of these are shared with other Celtic peoples such as the Irish, Scots, and Bretons. It seems that some traditions such as the Eisteddfod, the Cymanfa Ganu, and the Noson Lawen are peculiar to Wales. Of these, the eisteddfod remains the most popular. During recent years, however, the people of Wales have been celebrating St. David's Day in great style and in a variety of ways.

Saint David's Day (*Dydd Gŵyl Dewi Sant*): March 1: the feast day of Saint David, the patron saint of Wales, held in remembrance of the death of Saint David on that day in 587. March 1 was declared a national day of celebration within Wales in the 18th century. It is celebrated by Welsh societies throughout the world with dinners, parties, eisteddfodau, recitals and concerts. Welsh people wear a symbol of either a leek or daffodil. Every year parades are held in Wales to commemorate St. David. The largest of these is held in Cardiff, where the seventh National St. David's Day Parade takes place in the city centre, and where St David's Hall stages its traditional St David's Day concert. Swansea inaugurated a St David's Week festival in 2009 with a range of musical, sporting and cultural events to mark the national day. In Colwyn Bay in north Wales, an annual parade through the centre of town is now held with several hundred citizens and schoolchildren taking part. Other events are centred around the parade. In 2003 in the United States, St. David's Day was recognised officially as the national day of the Welsh, and on 1 March the Empire State Building is floodlit in the national colours, red, green and white.

The Eisteddfod (Chairing Ceremony): this is primarily a competition with the chief poetry contests for the Chair and for the Crown. The word *eisteddfod* itself means a session or "chairing" in which the winner is awarded a chair. The winners of local eisteddfodau (pl.) go on to compete on a county or regional level, eventually reaching the National Eisteddfod of Wales (Eisteddfod Genedlaethol Cymru) to compete with others from all over Wales. Here, the winner is crowned to great acclaim in a special ceremony conducted by the Gorsedd of Bards, led by the Archdruid of Wales.

The competition had its beginnings in the year 1176 when "... at Christmas in that year, the Lord Rhys ap Gruffudd held court in splendour at Cardigan (Aberteifi). And he set two kinds of contests there: one between bards and poets, another between harpists and crowders and pipers and various classes of music-craft. And he had two chairs set for the victors." This is the first known mention of the Eisteddfod, the festival that has become so much a part of Welsh culture and tradition and which has become, during the last decade, one of the largest folk festivals in Europe. There were eisteddfodau held during the reign of Queen Elizabeth 1st, mainly to license the activities of the Welsh bards, but they lapsed into obscurity until the latter part of the 18th Century when the London Welsh took advantage of the renewed interest in Britain regarding all things Celtic.

A Glamorgan stone mason, Edward Williams, known to posterity as Iolo Morganwg, helped create elaborate ceremonies that eventually led to those of today's National Eisteddfod of Wales. Since 1860-61, when the National Eisteddfod Society was founded, beginning the modern era of the competitions, the Eisteddfod has been presided over by the Gorsedd of Bards (Gorsedd Beirdd Ynys Prydain) founded by Iolo in 1792 in London. It made its first appearance at Carmarthen (at the Ivy Bush Hotel) in 1819 and has remained closely connected to the National ever since, being responsible for the elaborate and colourful ceremonies that accompany the introduction of new members as well as the awarding of the Crown and the Chair.

Today's Gorsedd of Bards (picture: chairing ceremony) is an association of poets, writers, musicians, artists and other individuals who have made a distinguished contribution to the Welsh nation, language, and culture. Members may not all be poets, but all have contributed greatly to Welsh life and culture. They can belong to one of three orders:

The Ovate Order (Green Robe) obtained by examination or by recommendation of the Gorsedd Board; the Order of Bards, Musicians and Literati (Blue Robe) the second step, obtained by passing the final Examination; and the Druidic Order (White Robe): restricted to those having made a substantial contribution of recognized national standard to Literature, Music, Scholarship or Art in Wales (or in Welsh societies overseas).

The Gorsedd emblem (called Awen) consists of three shafts of light in accord with the effect of the sun at different seasons, showing God's character as creator, sustainer and destroyer. The Gorsedd Stones, erected each year at a different venue, are set in alignment to the central Logan Stone, from where the Archdruid's solemn vows and announcement of that year's eisteddfod are spoken. At the Logan Stone are presented the Horn of Plenty (Hirlas), a sheaf of corn entwined with wild flowers, Blodeugedd) symbolizing the gift of the talents of Welsh Youth to the Archdruid), and the Floral Dance.

Today's Eisteddfod now includes arts and crafts, country dancing, folk singing, choral competitions, and drama and prose contests, all providing, a tremendous impetus to the fostering of Welsh as a living language. No English is allowed on the stage of the huge pavilion and choirs sometimes have to have pieces translated from other languages. The National Eisteddfod of Wales is held in a different venue each year during the first week in August.

Llangollen International Eisteddfod: The little town of Llangollen (the Church of St. Collen), is nestled snugly in the Dee Valley (Dyffryn Dyfrdwy) among high green hills. So near the border with England, the town has managed to retain much of its Welsh character, but for one week each July, the visitor might be excused for thinking he is in continental Europe. From one end to the other, the town will be crowded with dancers, singers, musicians and merrymakers from dozens of different nations, resplendent in national costumes.

A huge temporary pavilion houses the annual competitions for choirs and soloists, folk singers and dancers, musicians and special guests from the world of opera and show business. Not long after the War had finally ended, a brilliant idea came to the mind of an official of the British Council, Harold Tudor of Coedpoeth. Harold conceived the idea of an international folk festival, conducted very much along the lines of the Welsh National Eisteddfod, but open to competitors from all parts of the world.

Harold enlisted the support of the music organizer of the National, W. S. Gwynn Williams, who immediately welcomed the idea, especially as it would allow the people of Wales to contribute in their own unique manner to the healing of the terrible scars left by the War. And so it came to be that the first festival took duly took place in the summer of 1947 on the banks of the Dee, under the great hill crowned by the ancient Welsh castle of Dinas Bran.

The International Eisteddfod has been held each year since, attracting many thousands of spectators and hundreds of competitors, whose colorful native costumes and delightful singing and dancing fill the streets for one whole week (picture: folk dancers), transforming a little Welsh town into a miniature universe. In the pavilion, choirs from places as diverse as Ukraine, Morocco and Patagonia, and the United States meet in friendly competition. In recent years, the competitions have been augmented by "Choir of the Year" and "Singer of the Year" contests. The Choir of the world competition is open to male, female, and mixed choirs, attracting performers of a very high standard. The Singer of the Year brings outstanding soloists to Llangollen.

The Gymanfa Ganu (Singing Festival): another popular Welsh tradition, celebrated throughout Wales and by many Welsh Societies in

North America and elsewhere (though with the decline of the Chapel, it is losing some of its appeal to today's generation). The Cymanfa grew out of the Temperance Movement in Wales in the mid 19th century. In the chapels, certain days a year were set aside for the singing of hymns, led by conductors specially trained in bringing forth from their congregations the Welsh *hwyl* (deep-felt emotion). Many such "singing gatherings" include the huge event held in the Eisteddfod Pavilion on the last Sunday of National Eisteddfod Week in Wales and the North American National Gymanfa Ganu that began in Niagara Falls, New York, on Labour Day weekend in 1929. What began as a hymn-singing gathering has transformed itself into a National American Festival of Wales held over four days held in a different city in North America each year, including cities in Canada.

Christmas Eve Plygain: The Plygain is a survival of a pre-Reformation Christmas service modified to suit the new Protestant conditions, taking the place of the Catholic midnight Christmas and was originally associated with a communion service held later on Christmas morning. The Plygain itself was an abbreviated form of morning service interspersed with and followed by carols sung by soloists and parties. In many parts of Wales, Christmas meant rising early (or staying up overnight) to attend the Plygain service at the parish church. Often each person brought his or her candle to help to light the church.

The brilliant illumination from the candles of the attenders was an important feature of the festival. In Llanfyllin, special candles known as Canhwyllau Plygain were made by local chandlers in the middle of the nineteenth century. The spiritual significance of candle lighting at Christmas is a symbol of the coming of the Light of the World

As a general custom, the early-morning Christmas Plygain gradually died out, but it survived in some parishes. There, for almost two hours, the service is completely in the hands of the carol singers, who sing between twenty and thirty Christmas carols, all in Welsh and all different, since it is a point of honour not to offer a carol already heard that evening.

Hei Calennig: The giving of gifts on New Year's Day is an ancient custom. In Wales it took the form of collecting *calennig* (New Year's Gift). Children would form groups and go from house to house, bearing good wishes for the health and prosperity of the family during the year to come. This was symbolised by the skewered apples, stuck with corn and sprigs of evergreen, which they carried in their hands. Verses were sung at the door of the house, and they would receive small gifts of food or money for their troubles. The carrying of the apples has gradually been replaced by the reciting of a few verses in exchange for new pennies in those districts where it has survived.

The Noson Lawen (Merry Evening): This great Welsh tradition is of unknown age. It was originally held to celebrate the bringing in of the hay harvest, always a big event because of the uncertain Welsh weather. Festivities included *penillion* (the reciting of verses to the sound of the harp), dancing, and recitation. No doubt prodigious quantities of ale and cider were also consumed. The Noson Lawen gives everyone a chance to show his or her talents in village halls throughout Wales sometimes presided over by a professional Master of Ceremonies and keeps pace with the local eisteddfod as a living reminder of an older cultural tradition.

Shrove Tuesday: In many areas of Wales, Shrove Tuesday (Dydd Mawrth Ynyd) is an important reminder of ancient traditions. It was the last day upon which feasting, drinking and merriment could take place before the solemnities and fasting of Lent began. The Festival is also called Pancake Day for the last supplies of butter and fat were made into pancakes (*crempogau*). Naturally, plenty of eggs were used as well, and woe betide the unfortunate hen that failed to lay an egg before noon.

In Kidwelly (Cydweli), on the eve of Shrove Tuesday, tin cans were kicked up and down the streets. This was probably to commemorate the duty of putting away all pots and pans associated with the more abundant and tastier food that was forbidden during Lent. In a few areas, the Christmas decorations were not taken down on *Twelfth Night*, but remained until Shrove Tuesday, when they were removed and burned during the pancake feast. On this day, too, the poor people of the village went around from door to door begging for gift of flour and lard in order to make their own pancakes, for no house was to be without crempogau.

Palm Sunday (Sul y Blodau: Flower Sunday): Known in the Welsh-speaking districts of Wales as *Sul y Blodau* (Sunday of the Flowers), on this day it is the custom to decorate the graves in the churchyards with beautiful and fanciful flower arrangements as a preparation for the festival of the Resurrection. After the darkness and drabness of winter, as well as the solemnity of Lent, it was also the time to put on new clothes. Graves are often cleaned, weeded, and whitewashed before being decked with garlands of such plants as rosemary, rue, crocuses, daffodils and primroses in fanciful displays and patterns.

Good Friday (Gwener y Groglith): Good Friday was formerly known as *God Friday* in English, but the Welsh words translate as Friday of the Crucifixion). Various customs are associated with this day in Wales. Some of the more well- documented ones come from Tenby, in Southwest Wales. Business of every kind was totally suspended on this day, with no horse or cart (and very few people) to be seen on the streets at any hour. People also walked barefoot to church, so as not to "disturb the earth" the sacred burial ground of Christ.

On the same day, also in Tenby, the custom was long held of "making Christ's bed." Reeds were gathered from the riverbank and woven by young people into the shape of a human figure. The woven "Christ" was then laid on a wooden cross and left in a quiet part of a field or pasture to rest in peace. After the solemnity of Lent, the resurrection of the earth at Easter has always played an important part in Welsh tradition.

Hills and mountains have played their roles in the observance of Welsh customs throughout the centuries and the festivities on Easter Day are no exception. In many parts of the country, the celebrations for this most joyful of days begins before sunrise with a procession to the top of the nearest mountain. Crowds of people climb up to the highest point in the area to watch the sun "dance" as it rises through the clouds in honor of the resurrection of Christ.

In Llangollen, in the Vale of Clwyd, villagers used to greet the arrival of the sun's rays on the top of *Dinas Bran* (a location famous for its inclusion in many medieval Welsh folk tales) by dancing three somersaults. Nowadays, a pilgrimage to the top of the mountain is sufficient celebration. In other areas, a basin of water was taken to the top of the nearest hill to catch the reflection of the sun "dancing" on the horizon. Another favorite spot in Northeast Wales for this Easter festivity is the summit of *Moel Fammau*, in the Clwydian hills.

Cadi Haf: The first day of May in Wales is known as *Calan Mai* or *Calan Haf,* the first day of summer, in the same way that the first of November was known as *Calan Gaeaf,* the first day of winter. The celebrations always began the evening before, May Eve being one of the *ysprydnos* or 'spirit nights' (along with the evening before November 1st and St John's Day) when all sorts of spirits and supernatural forces were abroad, and divination was carried out with the aim of discovering who one's sweetheart would be.

On *Nos calan Mai* or May Eve, the villagers would go gathering hawthorn (*draenen wen,* literally whitethorn) branches and flowers which they would then use to decorate the outside of their houses. It was unlucky to bring hawthorn blossoms into the house. In other parts of Wales it was the Mayflower (probably the cowslip, *briallu Mair)* that was gathered, or rowan *(cerdinen)* and birch *(bedwen)* twigs. These customs celebrated the new growth and fertility of the season.

In the North, there was a custom called the *Cangen Haf,* whereby up to 20 young men would go May dancing, all of them dressed in white decorated with ribbons, except for two who were called the Fool and *Cadi* (an effeminate male figure in a man's coat and woman's petticoat) or *Cadi'r haf.* Other accounts mention only the Cadi who took on the role of "marshal, orator, buffoon and money collector." The significance of the Cadi, a figure who is neither man nor woman but partakes of both, is that of a figure who looks both ways and is therefore a transitional figure, fitting at this time in the cycle of the year when a new season is being ceremonially ushered in.

The *Cadi* or the Fool would carry the *cangen haf*, decorated with silver watches, spoons, and vessels borrowed from the village folk. There were usually around 12 dancers with a harpist or fiddler or both, who went from house to house dancing and singing and afterwards asking for a contribution of money.

Through the summer months in some Welsh villages, the people would gather on the *twmpath chwarae* (literally, tump for playing), the village green, in the evenings to dance and play various sports. The green was usually situated on the top of a hill and a mound was made where the fiddler or harpist sat. Sometimes branches of oak decorated the mound and the people would dance in a circle around it. *Dawnsio Haf,* summer dancing, was a feature of the May Day celebration, as was carolau *Mai,* May carols, also known as *carolau haf,* summer carols or *canu dan y pared,* singing under the wall. The singers would visit families on May morning accompanied by a harpist or fiddler, to wish them the greetings of the season and give thanks to "the bountiful giver of all good gifts." If their singing was thought worthy, they would be rewarded with food, drink, and possibly money. The custom came to a halt in many areas during or just after World War 11 but has recently been revived in Holywell, Flintshire (it may have begun in the village of Bagillt, nearby).

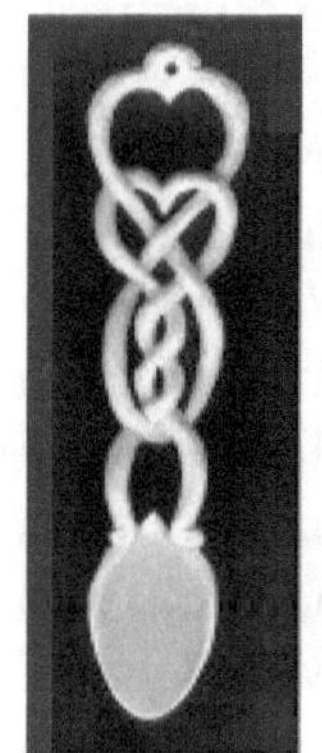

Llwy Caru (The Love Spoon): Though the custom of presenting various wooden articles as gifts was widespread in many countries of Europe from the end of the 17th Century, the giving of hand-made wooden love-spoons to one's sweetheart (or intended lover) seems to be a peculiarly Welsh custom, In Wales, the wooden articles took the form of intricately decorated spoons, given by the suitor as a prelude to courtship and a token of his interest. The carving of love spoons from a single piece of wood became a special pastime enjoyed by the peasantry in the long, idle winter months. As in many other customs, the eating of food seems to have a lot to do with the choice of a spoon as a gift.

The practice of using a particular utensil to eat led perhaps to the spoon's being chosen, first for its utilitarian use, then later as a symbol of a desire to help one's lover. The spoons were given long handles and could be hung on the wall as reminders or as decorations. Welsh love spoons began to appear in every conceivable size and shape and in different kinds of wood. Many produced today are made by a number of craftsmen anxious to show off their skills and imagination.

Many spoons were given as Valentines, and have the heart or entwined hearts motif; some have initials of the lovers. Some were made as puzzle spoons, with captive spheres or balls being carved in the handles. The finest display of love-spoons is now on permanent display, along with their history and areas of manufacture, at the Welsh Folk Museum, *St. Ffagans.*

The Leek: The leek is one of the national emblems of Wales, worn along with the daffodil (in Welsh, the daffodil is known as "Peter's Leek," Cenhinen Bedr) on St. David's Day. According to one legend, King Cadwaladr of Gwynedd ordered his soldiers to identify themselves by wearing the leek on their helmets in a battle against the Saxons. Legend or not, the leek has been a symbol of Wales for a long time; Shakespeare refers to the custom of wearing a leek as an "ancient tradition" in *Henry V.* In the play, Henry tells Fluellen that he is wearing a leek "for I am Welsh, you know, good countryman." The 1985 and 1990 British one pound coins bear the design of a leek in a coronet, representing Wales. Perhaps the most visible use of the leek, however, is as the cap badge of the Welsh Guards, a regiment within the Household Division of the British Army.

The Mari Lwyd: An ancient custom still practiced in a few villages and also being revived in many parts of Wales where it had been lost. Formerly known as *Aderyn Bee y Llwyd* (Bird with the grey beak," it involves using a horse's skull stuck on a pole covered with a white sheet and colored ribbons carried about town by a man crouched beneath the sheet. The party includes other characters singing verses from door to door requesting permission to enter. The householders then reply in verse in an impromptu competition until the callers are admitted for a session of revelry and a feast.

The Welsh Harp (Y Delyn Cymraeg): No Welsh festival of any kind would be complete without the attendance of a harpist, playing either the smaller native harp or the larger triple harp, with its three rows of strings. The triple harp may have been introduced from Italy in the early 18th Century but it has come to be regarded as national instrument of Wales. Some Welsh harpists play "gypsy style," with the harp on the left shoulder, a method favored by the Wood family of North Wales (*Teulu Abram Wood*).

The harp is the instrument favoured at Eisteddfodau, where the winner of the Crown is accompanied to the stage by the playing of a song of welcome to the ancient tune "Rhyfelgwrch Capten Morgan." It is not uncommon to see and hear choirs of harps at some of Wales's important music festivals. Once played by professional musicians in the homes of the gentry, the native harp was restored to popularity during the late Victorian period and has undergone something of a recent revival; many expert harpists are in much demand with orchestras and folk groups. One type of singing called *Penillion* is always accompanied by a harp.

Perhaps the most famous harpist of the Modern Era was Nansi Richards. (*Telynores Maldwyn*, 1888-1979). Nansi learned her craft from renowned harpist John Roberts, one of the "Children of Abram Wood." She passed on the knowledge of gypsy harping and their tunes to Llio Rhydderch and others(depicted: modern Welsh harpist).Other wonderful harpists are internationally known Elinor Bennett, and her protégé, Catrin Finch chosen by Prince Charles to be the Royal Harpist.

Hunting the Wren: This ancient cerermony is celebrated on December 26, St. Stephen's Day. Originally, a band of small boys known as *Wrenboys* hunted down a real wren, until they either caught it, or killed it. The boys would then carry it around the town, singing and asking for donations. The money was used to host a dance for the town, held that night. A pole decorated with ribbons, wreaths, and flowers was the center of the dance. The bird was put on top of the pole. The tradition now consists of "hunting" a fake wren, and putting it on top of a decorated pole. Boys celebrate the Wren by dressing up in masks, straw suits and colourful clothing and parade through the towns and villages in remembrance of a much older druidic festival. The live bird was eventually replaced with a fake one, hidden rather than chased. The money that is collected is usually donated to a school or charity. A celebration is still held around the decorated pole. Some people theorise that the Wren celebration has descended from Celtic mythology. The Druids used the wren in augury and might have studied its flight, amongst other birds, to derive predictions about the future. The wren was also blamed for betraying the Christian martyr Saint Stephen, after whom the day is named and therefore hunted and killed on St. Stephen's Day (the celebration is observed on the Isle of Man, Ireland, and Newfoundland as well as Wales).

The Madog Legend: After the accession to the throne of Henry Tudor (Henry VII) and the integration of Wales into the realm of Britain by his son, Henry VIII, there was a sudden surge of interest in the ancient land. Through revisions of ancient works, the wonderful tales of Geoffrey of Monmouth, concocted from his imagination as they might have been, were resurrected. They retained their powerful hold on the Welsh consciousness, enabling them to hold on to the idea that they, and they alone in the whole of Britain were the true British race and the rightful heirs to the Arthurian tradition. As scholar John Davies of Hereford stated in 1590: "We have long been afflicted and oppressed by those that sought our whole race to destroy," adding, "Caerleon, where King Arthur lived of yore shall be rebuilt and double gilt once more." Queen Elizabeth's interest was kindled.

When she felt it would benefit her rule, Elizabeth took full advantage of her Welsh ancestry. She authorized the translation of the Bible into Welsh, a good way to ensure that Protestantism took a firm hold on the land of her ancesters, but also in an attempt for them to learn English by having bibles in both languages placed side by side in church. She also encouraged the writings of London Welshman John Dee, a key figure in the expansion of her island kingdom overseas.

Dee publicized the traditions involving Prince Madog of Gwynedd's supposed discovery of the New World during the 12th century when he brought his little fleet into what is now Mobile Bay, Alabama. The legend has him exploring the Mississippi Valley and joining the Mandan tribe, whose pitifully few remnants are said to still revere a white ancestor.

Elizabeth's court officials eagerly seized the legend, diligently promoting attempts to find the Northwest Passage to India as justification for their war against the Spanish, and proof of their legitimate claims to the Americas. Dee's preposterous claims included King Arthur's ruling over large territories in the Atlantic, and that Madog's voyage had confirmed the Welsh (and therefore Tudor) title to this empire. As successor to the Welsh princes, Elizabeth was thus the rightful sovereign of the Atlantic Empire.

Another surge of interest in the history of the mysterious people who continued to use their ancient Celtic language and to practice their ancient customs took place in the late 18th century. In 1792, an address by Sir William Jones re-established the ancient claim that North America had been discovered by Prince Madog 300 years before the voyage of Columbus. Jones praised the so-called "Welsh Indians," descended from Madog and his fellow explorers, a "free and distinct people, who have preserved their liberty, languages, and some traces of their religion to this very day."

Fresh interest in the Madoc legend was thus rekindled in Britain. An account was published in London in 1790 by John Williams, encouraged by the indefatigable Iolo Morgannwg (who had invented many "authentic" Celtic customs). Thus, in 1792, John Thomas Evans of Waunfawr, Caernarfon decided to search for the Welsh Indians. His journey was unsuccessful, though his explorations of the Missouri

Valley led to that territory being charted for the first time. His maps were a great help to the later expeditions of Lewis and Clark.

A letter of John Williams to the Cymmrodorion Socety in 1797 denied the existence of the Welsh Mandans, and an 1858 essay of Thomas Stephens gave little credence to the story. Nonetheless, whatever the facts behind it, it has remained a beloved story and a source of national pride, helping to restore an almost lost sense of pride and dignity. While working in India with the East India Company, Sir William also discovered the connection (hitherto unknown) between the Celtic languages and Sanskrit, the ancient language of Indian holy books. The Welsh language was thus given an honored place in history, a full partner in the Indo-European family of languages.

Male Voice Choirs (Corau Meibion): No final word on Welsh traditions can omit the famous Male Voice Choirs, still very much part of the nation's heritage though sadly in decline during the last few years. In South Wales, the Temperance Movement of the 1830's first gave impetus to choral singing, and in 1846, choral competition was added to the events at the Aberdare National Eisteddfod. A medal was awarded to choral singing at Swansea in 1867 and the Welsh Valleys in particular were full of great choirs, including the South Wales Choral Union, winners at Crystal Palace in 1872 and 1873. Welsh pioneers to Utah began a choir at Salt Lake City as soon as they arrived in 1847 that grew into the world-famous Mormon Tabernacle Choir. In the Wales of today, the Eisteddfod still holds competitions for Male Voice choirs though most of the larger ones, such as the Morriston Orpheus, Pendyrus, Treorchy Male Voice, Rhos Orpheus etc, no longer compete, preferring to use their talents in concerts.

Chapter Seven: The Princes of Wales (Tywysogion Cymru)

Following the Statute of Rhuddlan (The Statute of Wales) in 1284, Edward began his massive castle-building program. With the help of the architect Master James of St. George, and with what must have seemed like limitless resources in labor and materials, Edward placed a stranglehold on the Welsh. In 1301 King Edward of England made seventeen-year-old Lord Edward his eleventh son [born in 1284 to Elinor at Caernarfon Castle], "Prince of Wales and Count of Chester," and ever since that date these titles have been automatically conferred upon the first-born son of the English monarch. The Welsh people had very little say in the matter. As Elinor given birth to her son in Wales, there is a story that they were duped into paying homage to a boy "who spoke no English and who was born in Wales."

In the long years of Welsh history before King Edward's proclamation, because of intense personal rivalry between petty kingdoms, only five Welsh princes could justify their claim to be truly rulers of Wales. These were Rhodri Mawr (Rhodri the Great), Hywel Dda (Hywel the Good, Gruffudd ap Llywelyn, Llywelyn ap Iorwerth (Llywelyn the Great), and Llywelyn ap Gruffudd (Llywelyn the Last).

The first investiture of the English Prince of Wales took place at Lincoln in 1301, far away from Wales. In 1346, Edward the Prince of Wales (the Black Prince), son of Edward 111, adopted the *Three Feathers* from the plume of John, King of Bohemia, whom he slew at the Battle of Crecy. Along with it, he took the German motto "Ich Dien" (I Serve). It was not until 1400 that a native Welshman, Owain Glyndwr, a wealthy landowner from Sycharth, in the Dee Valley, North east Wales, proclaimed himself Prince of Wales, first at Glyndyfrdwy (the Dee Valley), and again at Machynlleth the same year, where he had summoned a Welsh Parliament.

In 1404, Owain was officially crowned before representatives from Castille, France and Scotland. He was the last Welshman to claim the title. When his rebellion ultimately ended in 1413, Wales reverted to English rule. Since that time, the title Prince of Wales has had very little meaning for the people of Wales. In 1632, a petition by Dr. John Davies to have the young Prince of Wales learn Welsh was ignored. During the reign of Queen Victoria, a half-hearted proposal again surfaced in the House of Commons to have the infant Prince of Wales instructed in the Welsh language. It was ridiculed in the national newspapers and the idea came to nought.

The modern investiture ceremonies began under the inspiration of the self-serving Welshman Lloyd George, then Chancellor, who had Edward crowned in a sort of medieval nonsense at Caernarfon in 1911 (the same Edward who was to renounce his throne). Another ceremony took place at Caernarfon in 1969, when Prince Charles, heir to the throne, announced his allegiance to Wales and promised as "liege lord" to protect his realm from "all manner of foes." Since that non-event, for which Charles prepared by studying the Welsh language at Aberystwyth University, he has spent very little time in Wales, which has no Royal Palace or residence.

The Princess of Wales: Lady Diana Spencer (1961-1997) was the first holder in history to attach any real importance to the title of Princess of Wales or to make effective use of it. As far as I know, very few, if any indexes in a history of Great Britain (or Wales) have an entry for "Princess of Wales," regardless of whether the title holder was Welsh-born or not. After her divorce from Prince Charles in 1996, Diana became internationally known for her work in a multitude of charitable and humane causes, including her personal crusade against anti-personnel land mines, visiting Angola and Bosnia; She also worked closely with AIDS organizations and charities for children. Sadly, Lady Di, as she was affectionately known, was killed in a car crash in Paris while escaping photographers.

Chapter Eight: The Changing Faces of Welsh Industry

Beginning around the middle of the 18th century, parts of Wales experienced an explosion of mining, quarrying, iron manufacturing and all their related industries. In northwest Wales, on the green, unspoiled island of Anglesey, the huge Mona and Parys copper mines helped transform both the economy and the landscape: copper smelting employed hundred of workmen and poisoned the hillsides around Amlwch. In the ancient kingdom of Gwynedd, huge quarries also began to disfigure the landscape, but employed thousands of men to dig out the slate that roofed houses and municipal buildings throughout Europe.

Collieries at Flint and Bagillt; iron foundries at Mostyn, on the Dee estuary; the beginnings of extensive coal mining at Llay, Gresford, and Point of Ayr; and the pioneering John Wilkinson iron works at Bersham, near Wrexham also helped make that corner of Wales a center of industry. In Southeast Wales, the coming of industry completely changed the landscape and the way of life.

The bituminous or semi-bituminous coals of the Welsh Valleys solved the problem of the scarcity of charcoal: they provided an extremely valuable, readily available fuel in prodigious quantities. Some of the major producers were John Guest, associated with the Dowlais and Plymouth works; Anthony Bacon and William Brownrigg, who began the Cyfartha Works; Richard Crawshay, who later bought and expanded Cyfartha; and the Homfrays, who owned Penydarren.

By 1827, the South Wales iron industry was producing one half of all Britain's iron exports, much of it to the United States. Rapidly-growing Swansea became the chief copper producer of Britain, if not the world. Before the end of the nineteenth century, all this feverish activity meant that Wales was about to be transformed from a quiet backwater on the western edge of Europe to one of the foremost centers of industry in the world in a few short years. It possessed what Ireland did not —- coal. Along with industrialization came a dramatic increase in the numbers of inhabitants— from approximately 500,000 people in the 1750's to over 1,600,000 in 1851 and 2,600,000 before Word War One.

The movement into the five great valleys of the South was so great that Wales ranked second to the United States as a world center of immigration in the latter half of the nineteen century (pictured: a Welsh miner with a pit pony). At the Ynyscedwyn Iron Works in Ystradgynlais, David Thomas opened up the West Wales coalfield by making it possible to use anthracite coal in the smelting of iron ore. In the Merthyr district the great iron works of Cyfartha, Pen y Darren and Blaenavon produced a major share of British Iron, and at Dowlais was made practically the sum total of all iron rails for the fledgling United States railroad industry. South of Merthyr, and greatly profiting from its heavy industry and relentless toil of its workers, was Cardiff, its outlet to the sea at the bottom of the five valleys (Rhymney, Rhonda, Cynon, Taff, and Ebbw) and the main center of export to the overseas empire. Cardiff exported more coal than any other port in the world, up to 40 percent of British exports and 25 percent of world exports.

The "Great Unrest" in the early years of the 20th Century was felt throughout the industrialized world. In Wales, it manifested itself most prominently in two areas. In the North, The growth of unionism was fiercely resisted by Lord Penrhyn, who demanded absolute submissiveness and obedience from the workers in the numerous slate quarries on his estates. The workers struck on 22 November 1900 in what was to become the longest-lasting dispute in British history, and one that ended in complete defeat for the quarrymen.

By the time World War I began, cheaper and more accessible roofing materials were entering the world markets. The slate industry, at its peak employing 18,000 men, and a pillar of the Welsh language community in North Wales, never recovered. It was in the South, however, because of the vast numbers of workers involved, that the Great Unrest produced the most dramatic results.

The War spelled the end of Britain's dominance of world affairs. There was simply too much reliance on the traditional industries of cotton, coal mining and shipbuilding, all of which were finding it difficult to compete in world markets, and all of which were managed by those who could not adapt to more modern methods. Coal hung on desperately for quite some time as the largest Welsh industry. Yet the numbers employed in its production fell to 115,000 by 1947, a drop of 150,00 in just over twenty years. The majority of Welsh mines were old and practically exhausted; seams were irregular and hard to cut; machinery and production methods were out of date. The nationalization of industry in Britain began in 1947, the central boards taking over administration of all industry in Wales. The National Coal Board closed down all inefficient mines, modernized and centralized others.

Steel found itself temporarily revitalized by huge new concerns at Margam, in Glamorganshire; at Shotton, in Flintshire; and at Ebbw Vale in Monmouthshire, the three huge new plants producing over a quarter of all Britain's steel. The government also invested heavily at Britain's finest natural harbor, Milford Haven, where new oil refineries were established. In Anglesey and Snowdonia, nuclear and hydroelectric power stations were built to provide for the large English cities and industries in the Midlands and North. In places such as Newtown, in Powys, light industries were introduced, with dozens of factories setting up shop in the ubiquitous industrial parks that began to transform the landscapes in the 1960's as well as the lives of the people who came to work in them.

Heavy industry, in which Britain had led the world for so long, continued its decline. Australia's sale to Japan of nearly six million tons of iron ore from the Hamersly Range deposits in 1964 allowed a major expansion of the Japanese steel industry, making her an industrial superpower and practically spelling the end of the Welsh steel industry. In the 1980's, Ebbw Vale alone lost over 10,000 jobs its steel plants. By the beginning of the 1980's, the economy and the society of Wales were far different than they had been in 1945. Not one single working pit remained in the Rhondda Valley, which had been synonymous with coal for over a hundred years. The Five Valleys lost much of their sense of community as commuting to Cardiff and Newport became a way of life.

In the latter years of the 20th Century, Britain finally came to terms with the loss of much of its heavy industry and the increasing reliance on finance, communications, oil, insurance, tourism, accounting and other service industries. The economy began to recover; inflation was at a 30-year low. The sale of tens of thousands of public housing (at bargain prices) put the country far ahead of the U.S. and Europe in the percentage of housing units owner-occupied. Britain had the highest growth rate and the lowest unemployment in Europe. Wales did not fully share in the bounty, but the creation of the Welsh Assembly in 1999 and its Welsh Development Agency have been attracting new industries, many from the U.S., Japan, and Korea.

Chapter Nine: Wales Emigration to America:

Following the Act of Uniformity in 1662, Welsh Baptists under John Myles founded a church at Swanzey, Massachusetts, the first church in the American Colonies to be founded by a Welshman. Other religious groups were troubled by the measures to ensure conformity enforced by the English Parliament after the return of the Stuart Monarchy. The Quakers, the Society of Friends, sought lands where they could practice their own form of religion and where they could live under their own laws in a Welsh Barony; they were quickly followed by Baptist congregations as well as many other religious groups.

The Quaker project, envisioned as a kind of "Holy Experiment," involved an oral understanding with William Penn and the Society of Friends that 40,000 acres of land in southeastern part of what later became Pennsylvania (some sources give 30,000) were to be set aside as this Barony. Unfortunately, this agreement was never put into writing. Penn himself was not Welsh (his ancestors may have been from Wales before settling in Ireland). In 1690, however, to the dismay of the Welsh settlers, the Colonial government abolished the civil authority of the Welsh Quaker meetings in order to set up regular town government.

Welsh settlements had begun to spread out, on the west side of the Schuylkill River. The St.David's Society of Philadelphia was begun in 1729, and thus it is the oldest ethnic society of its kind in the US. One prominent member was Robert Morris, credited with financing the American Revolution. Since its founding, it has provided many men of distinction throughout the ensuing centuries, making their influence felt in politics, agriculture, and the administration of justice, as well as in industry, particularly mining and the manufacturing of iron and steel.

According to the Society, 16 signers of the Declaration of Independence were of Welsh descent: George Clymer, Stephen Hopkins, Robert Morris, William Floyd, Francis Hopkinson, John Morton, Britton Gwinnett, Thomas Jefferson, John Penn, George

Read, John Hewes, Francis Lewis (born in Wales), James Smith, Williams Hooper, Lewis Morris, and William Williams (there are many historians who may dispute these names, but the majority of the persons listed have at least some Welsh connections).

In 19th century a steady migration took from the rural districts of Wales to the rapidly growing industrial towns of Glamorganshire and Monmouthshire; and to England. Others crossed the ocean to upper New York State, to Pennsylvania, to Ohio, and to other areas in the United States. In 1839 David Thomas arrived in Allentown from Ystradgynlais where he had been steward of the Ynyscedwyn Iron Works. His success in smelting iron ore with anthracite set off a stream of emigration from Wales, mostly ironworkers or coal miners mainly to Pennsylvania, but also to Ohio and W. Virginia. Additional emigration took place after the United States Government passed the McKinley Tariff Act of 1891 that had a drastic effect on the Welsh tinplate industry, leading to closures of many factories and to massive unemployment.

The Welsh chapels of such towns as Scranton, Wilkes-Barre, Pittston, Hazelton, Minersville, Edwardsville, Slatington, Delta, and others in eastern Pennsylvania as well as those in Vermont and Allegany County, Maryland attest to the influence of the newcomers in those predominantly coal and slate-mining areas. At one time, there were approximately 30,000 people of Welsh descent in the Scranton area where many of their Welsh chapels survive. Some of these chapels continue to hold Welsh hymn-singing festivals (*Cymanfaoedd Ganu*) yearly, and there are Welsh societies in the majority of the states of the Union.

At Edwardsville, Pennsylvania, there is an annual eisteddfod begun in 1889 that continues to attract wide interest. In Gallia County, Ohio, many Welsh families were forced to stay when their raft containing all their possessions drifted away in the night. At Oak Hill, a small museum is dedicated to the many Welsh who settled and worshipped in the area during the late 19th century.

Many Welsh families went to Le Seueur and Blue Earth Counties in Minnesota, where an annual Gymanfa Ganu takes place in St. Peter. Even further west, in Oregon, the Bryn Seion Church at Beavercreek holds a Gymanfa each June that attracts many worshippers from other states. At Los Angeles, California, the Welsh Presbyterian Church still struggles to survive, but during the 1990's had something of a revival and has sponsored many Welsh events, including two Cymanfaoedd Ganu yearly and a St. David's Day Concert. A most professional and most successful Welsh choir has also been recently created in southern California. It is Utah, however, that has the highest percentage of Welsh Americans of any state.

During the middle years of the 19th century, Missionary activity in Wales led to the formation of many branches the Church of Latter Day Saints (Mormons). of the movement and to the emigration of 249 members on the *Buena Vista* from Liverpool in May 1849. They were led by Captain Dan Jones, a Welshman who had been very active in taking American converts to Salt Lake City.

Over three hundred newly-arrived Welsh converts left Iowa City in June, 1849 pushing hand-carts with their belongings to begin the long trek to Salt Lake City. They sang as they journeyed. Less than two weeks after their arrival, they began to form permanent choirs in a temporary meetinghouse, a log structure known as "The Bowery." The very first program of the choir that was to become the famous Mormon Tabernacle choir took place on Sunday, August 22, 1847. Under some skilled and demanding Welsh conductors, it was to reach the highest possible standards in the world of choral music.

In the past few years, just as in Wales itself there have been many attempts to revive the ancient culture, the same phenomenon has been taking place in North America. A National Cymanfa Ganu (begun at Niagara Falls in 1929) held in a different city each Labor-Day weekend that attracts thousands of Welsh-Americans and Canadians for a four-day celebration of Welsh culture, centered around a full day of hymn-singing, but including many more activities in a Festival of Wales.

An annual Welsh Heritage Week and a Welsh Language Week have been going strong for a number of years now, held in a different state or province each summer (and sometimes in Wales itself). An annual conference attracts many distinguished scholars of Welsh and Welsh-American studies to such college campuses such as that of Bryn Mawr, Pennsylvania; Rio Grande, Ohio; and West Virginia University.

Welsh-American societies include the N.W.A.F. (the National Welsh-American Foundation), which recognizes prominent Welsh-Americans, publishes books on Wales and the Welsh in the U.S, distributes an informative newsletter (*The Eagle and the Dragon)* grants scholarships and supports projects on both sides of the Atlantic. Cymdeithas Madog sponsors an annual Welsh Language Week and other activities. The N.W.G.G.A (the National Welsh Gymanfa Ganu Association) sponsors an annual Festival of Wales and also supports Welsh cultural activities through scholarships and grants. Other societies include the W.A.G.S (the Welsh -American Genealogical Society); and the Welsh home for the Aged, in Rocky River, Ohio. In addition, there is a Welsh-American newspaper, now a combined edition of *Y Drych* and *Ninnau.*

As a member of the British Commonwealth, Canada has also gained handsomely from its Welsh citizens. There are approximately 350,000 Welsh Canadians, with large Welsh societies in Vancouver, Ottowa, and Toronto. The latter city claims over 45,000 Welsh men and women. For over a century Toronto has celebrated St. David's Day with a festive dinner and organizes Welsh-related activities throughout the year.

But the Welsh emigrants in the U.S. and Canada were all too few to keep a completely separate identity. There was no great wave of immigration to the colonies from a country whose total population in the late 18th century hardly reached half a million. In 1770, in fact, Carmarthen's 4,000 inhabitants made it the largest town in Wales. We have therefore to consider the influence of those Welsh who did emigrate to North Amerca to be out of all proportion to their small numbers, a phenomenon repeated in Patagonia, Argentina and in the Australian sub-continent.

Chapter Ten: Welsh Patagonia

The most "successful" colony, in so far as maintaining its cultural identity is concerned, was that founded by a group of hardy pioneers in the most unlikely place — the Chubut Valley in the wastelands of Patagonia, Southern Argentina. At a meeting held in 1861 in Bala, North Wales, at the home of Michael D. Jones, a group of men discussed the possibility of founding the new Promised Land somewhere other than Wisconsin, or even Pennsylvania. These states had had held out so much promise at first, but in them the Welsh chapels and the Welsh language were becoming rapidly anglicized and the congregations divorced from their heritage.

For quite some time Michael Jones, recently returned from America, had felt that the U.S.A. offered the best hope for saving the Welsh nation from extinction, but by the 1860's his hope had vanished. The Welsh congregations in the United States were not keeping in touch with one another, although the Welsh-American newspaper *Y Drych* (which is still published monthly, but now in English) had been started in 1855 to try to establish connections between the far-too scattered Welsh-American communities. It was all too apparent that chances of a distinct Welsh identity in the U.S. were fading rapidly.

Jones, Principal of Bala College, elaborated on his dream. He had been corresponding with the Argentine government about settling the area known as Bahia Blanca in eastern Patagonia, where Welsh immigrants would be allowed to keep their language, their traditions and their self-identity.

In Wales itself, there was no Welsh political party; the established church was asleep as usual, doing nothing to preserve any sense of Welsh nationhood; the government of Great Britain in Westminster was apathetic if not hostile to Welsh concerns. No one seemed to care about the fate of the Welsh nation, still fighting desperately to survive after one thousand years of struggle. Now there was a new crisis: in the face of increasing Anglicization of their beloved land, for such as Michael Jones and a few other patriots, it seemed necessary for Welsh people to move away from Wales to preserve their heritage. As the Welsh in the United States were being swallowed up their neighbors, perhaps opportunities existed in South America. Thus negotiations began with Argentina.

The Argentine government, anxious to control a vast unpopulated area in which it was in dispute with the government of Chile, was willing to grant 100 square miles for the establishment of a Welsh state and to protect it by the military. A Welsh emigration committee, meeting in Liverpool (where there was a large Welsh population) the same year (1861), decided that here was a chance to fulfill a dream that could not be turned down. The committee decided to publish a handbook to advertise the undertaking, *Llawlyfr y Wladfa* ("Colony Handbook"), and to distribute it throughout Wales and in areas of Welsh settlement in the United States.

In 1862 Lewis Jones went to Buenos Aires, followed by Captain Jones-Parry to confirm the agreement with the government of Argentina, represented by Dr. Rawson, the minister of the interior (after whom the capital of the province of Patagonia is now named). In the U.S. the Welsh-American paper *Y Drych* warned its readers against the scheme to settle Patagonia, fearing troubles with the native Indian population.

As it happened, once the scheme got under way, the natives were the least of the emigrants' troubles. After many delays and problems with the ship initially chosen, the *Halton Castle*, a group of nearly 200 Welshmen and women sailed away from Liverpool in late May, 1865 to the promised land on the *Mimosa*, a brig of 447 tons. Blessed by fair weather and with the death of only five children in those days of calamitous on-board sickness (two children were born at sea) the ship arrived safely at what is now Puerto Madryn on the 27th day of July, 1865, landing its passengers the next day.

The area had previously been explored by Captain Fitzroy of the Royal Navy. He had called the landing place *New Bay* at the mouth of the river the Welsh were to call *Camwy* (swirling river). He had optimistically described the area as suitable for raising cattle and sheep with sufficient good land, fruit trees and water, and plenty of quality marble for mining. More important, however, the land was also offered free. Captain Fitzroy's descriptions notwithstanding, much of eastern Patagonia is a dusty, lonely land.

Today, the Camwy Valley is known as *Chubut*; like the Nile Valley in Egypt, it offers a thin strip of green, fertile and welcome tree-dotted land surrounded on both sides by the hostile scrub-filled semi-desert. The Chubut Valley is only 50 miles long, and its gray, sullen waters irrigate an area only 6 miles wide. Yet just as the Nile is known as the cradle of civilization in Egypt, so the Chubut Valley is the foundation of the Welsh settlement of Patagonia.

In 1853, Welshman Henry Libanus Jones had been in the Chubut area attempting to capture wild cattle. He built something of a fort with a few huts remaining when the *Mimosa* arrived offshore. Here, in a place they named Hen Amddiffynfa (*the old Fort*), the Welsh arrivals settled in, building new homes from river mud or sun-dried brick. Some settlers even occupied caves in the hills while they pondered how to cultivate the plots of land (124 acres each family or bachelor) granted by the Argentine government and allocated by the drawing of lots. It was not an easy task; water was scarce, food was in short supply; there were no forests as in Pennsylvania to provide abundant building supplies and wild game.

One group exploring the valley, and crazed with thirst, were forced to shoot a hawk to drink its blood. Window coverings were made from the stomach lining of the flightless rhea. Even the joyful birth of the first Welsh child in Patagonia, Mary Humphries, did little to dispel the belief of the settlers that they had made a mistake in coming to such a desolate, inhospitable location. The colony looked as if it were doomed to fail for lack of food.

A temporary respite from famine was made possible through the efforts of Lewis Jones, who brought a number of sheep, cattle, pigs, poultry and horses from Buenos Aires, along with some wheat, potatoes and blankets on the *Mary Ellen.* A diet of mutton salted with seawater helped fend off starvation. Further help came when the *Denby* arrived from Beunos Aires with more supplies later in the year. The settlers also benefited from cordial relations with the native Indians, the Teheulche, who showed up one day with their chief, curious to see what was going on.

It was the Teheulche who taught the Welsh how to catch the guanaco, rhea, and those other sources of food available on the prairie. The Indians would exchange meat for bread, going from house to house uttering the very first Welsh word they learned mixed with their Spanish to produce "poco bara" (a bit of bread). The meat was invaluable and ensured survival.

Despite the bounty provided by the supplies of meat, much suffering continued. Early trials, including many mistakes in misunderstanding the climate and the soil of the area led many to consider leaving Chubut altogether for a more northerly province. They were persuaded to stay by Lewis Jones and Abram Matthews.

In November, 1867 the situation improved: a ship brought much-needed supplies, but more importantly, Rachel Jenkins suggested to her husband that channels be built from the Chubut river to irrigate the land. She had noticed how the river sometimes burst its banks: their planted vegetables would benefit from water brought from the river. Many local historians see this as the one decision that changed the history of the colony.

Welsh hands toiled feverishly with whatever tools they could find to build the canals and dykes and pumping stations. The following spring saw a bountiful wheat harvest. Success meant that the government at Santa Fe took serious notice of the colony, and one immediate result was that Mr.Rawson sent additional food and livestock.

The Welsh had arrived in the desert and had been delivered. In a roughly -built barn that was used in Rawson as a public hall, Abram Matthews delivered the first sermon "Israel in the Wilderness." But more settlers were needed and the appeal went out. Additional immigrants, attracted by what was happening in Chubut arrived in 1875 and 1876, mainly from Wales but also from New York State. In 1877 a new chapel was opened in Gaiman with Minister John Evans in charge.

In 1880, land donated by some of the settlers was used for the building of *Moriah* Chapel in Trelew followed by *Tabernacl*, erected on land donated by the new Port Madryn Railway Company. This company had come into being to take agricultural products to Port Madryn for export. Funds for its construction had been raised in

Liverpool, and the necessary materials arrived in 1886 to build the railroad under the direction of builder Thomas Davies of Aberystwyth, and engineer Edward Williams of Mostyn, Flintshire. By 1888 Port Madryn had been connected by rail to Trelew (Welsh for Lewistown, named after Lewis Jones.)

A disastrous flood in 1899 wiped out many farms and halted progress on the railroad. It almost destroyed the colony, for three years later a sizeable number of Welsh families left for Canada, where there would be good land to farm. In Canada, too, they would be able to learn English in schools rather than Spanish, as was now being required by the Argentine government, going back on its original agreement with the early settlers.

Despite the loss of 234 settlers (whose journey to Winnipeg, Saskatchwan was funded by both the British and Canadian governments), a new era in the prosperity of the colony began when the rail was extended to Gaiman in 1909, to Dolavon in 1917. It eventually reached Las Plumas, the western end of the line that continued in operation until the 1960's. The rough period had come to an end, and the old dream of *Wladfa Gymreig* was fast becoming a reality.

A new chapel was built in Rawson, and *Bethel* Chapel was erected in Gaiman. The colony was extended westwards into the Andes region where Trevelyn and Esquel still hold Welsh Sunday Chapel services. A Welsh pioneer in the region, Llwyd ap Iwan, a son of Michael D. Jones, earned the dubious distinction as having been killed by a companion of famed outlaw Butch Cassidy in 1909. It was not just Chapel building however, in which the Welsh excelled (depicted: The Chubut Valley).

The vast distance between the colony and the central government led to the settlers soon establishing their own administration. They set up a system of government with a president, twelve councilors, a justice of the peace, a secretary, a treasurer and a registrar. For the first few years they even used a system of currency brought with them from Wales. The idea of bringing the eisteddfod to Chubut began at a gathering in 1876 at Beti Huws' farm; it became firmly established in Trelew in 1900.

Today, the Eisteddfod Mawr forms an important part in the life of the fast-growing town. A two-day event, it attracts competitors from all parts of Chubut and even farther afield. Like the eisteddfodau in Wales, there is a competition for the chair and the crown, the first being given for the best prose entry in Welsh, the second for the best poem in Spanish. The standards are quite high, and competition in all categories is fierce, especially in choral singing, with choirs (singing in Welsh and Spanish) coming from miles around.

Recent efforts to make sure the Welsh language stays alive in an area that has attracted thousands whose sole language is Spanish have seen the borrowing of teachers from Wales. For her work in fostering such attempts to preserve the Welsh heritage of Chubut, in 1999, Patagonian native Tegai Roberts received the coveted white robe of membership in the Gorsedd of Bards of Britain. According to Dafydd Iwan, who visited the area in 2001 and of the many teachers and tourists who have followed him since, evidence of Welsh culture is still very strong in Chubut, in far-off Patagonia.

Chapter Eleven: The Welsh in Australasia

After the U.S., and Patagonia, Australia beckoned the largest group of Welsh emigrants. Figures for Australians of Welsh descent are hard to come by: so many emigrants from Wales were simply classed as being from "England and Wales. " As in the U.S., however, Welsh people played a very important part in the development of their new country in many areas. In the early 1990's, about 30,000 Australians were Welsh-born, the majority arriving after the Second World War.

The first known Welsh people to arrive in Australia came on the "First Fleet" of 1788: they were convicts: two men and two women. Even before this time, however, Welsh crews were present on James Cook's voyages. The medical officer aboard the *Discovery* was Dafydd Ddu Feddyg (Black David the Doctor). In the 1830's more Welsh convicts arrived, including leaders of the Trade Union movement and the Merthyr Riots of 1831, including Lewis Lewis *(Lewsyn yr Heliwr*) who had been sentenced to death along with Richard Lewis (*Dic Penderyn*), but who had his sentence commuted to life imprisonment. They were followed by John Frost, Zephania Williams, and Charles Jones, exiled for their part in the Newport Rising of 1839. One of the most famous of all Welsh emigrants, whose exploits as "the jolly swagman" of song earned him a prominent place in the pantheon of Australian folk heroes, was Joseph Jenkins, who left Cardiganshire because of a nagging wife.

The Australian Gold Rushes of the 1850's attracted a number of Welshmen (and women). Many copper miners had already helped settle the new colony of South Australia. William Meirion Evans of Llanfrothen, Merioneth, is believed to have been the first person to hold religious services on the Australian continent in the Welsh language when he preached at Burra in 1849. Evans also founded and edited the Welsh-language periodicals *Yr Awstralydd* ("the Australian") and *Yr Ymwelydd* ("the Visitor").

The gold fields of Victoria brought many miners to the Ballaret-Sebastopol area. Welshmen became political leaders, business managers and storeowners. David Jones, from North Wales became owner of the largest drapery store in the area. David John Thomas became Melbourne's most eminent surgeon and founded the Melbourne Hospital. As in other territories, the Welsh set up their chapels almost as soon as they arrived, and the eisteddfodau, cymanfaoedd ganu and other Welsh cultural activities.

In New South Wales, Edgeworth David discovered and developed the major coal seams, and another David Jones (of Llandeilo, Carmarthenshire) became the leading draper of all Australia. Coal was also a magnet for many Welsh to move into Queensland in the 1860's. On the Ipswich Coalfield, a vigorous Welsh community established itself in the town of Blackstone. Lewis Thomas, of Talybont, Cardiganshire became known as the King of the Queensland coalfields. His house, B*rynhyfryd*, became a centre of Welsh cultural activities for many years. The Blackstone Eisteddfod was begun in 1887. The modern Australia-wide Eisteddfod movement derives from these beginnings; they have developed into well-recognized breeding grounds for the nurturing of musical and artistic talents throughout the country.

Welsh people in Australia have also made their presence felt most strongly in industry and politics. As in Pennsylvania, their long experience in mining helped them to become foremen, engineers, and draughtsmen as well as workers on the coalface. In the two developments that have shaped much of the history of modern Australia, Welshmen were important: the Federation and the Australian Labour Party. The principal architect of the Federal Constitution was Sir Samuel Walker Griffith from Merthyr Tydfil; an early leader of the Labour movement and Prime Minister of Australia from 1915-23 was William Morris Hughes (the Little Digger); and the first Labour Premier of South Australia was Welsh-born Thomas Price. In many other areas of Australian life, Welsh men and women have played important, if unheralded roles.

As in so many other areas in the world where Welsh have settled, gradual dispersion into the general population has meant a decline in their cultural activities. There are very few chapels in Australia that still continue to offer services in the Welsh language. To cater to a belated Celtic revival, however, some Australian radio stations offer programs about Wales and even offer Welsh language classes, and many cities continue to conduct annual Cymanfaoedd Ganu and eisteddfodau with the proceedings mostly in English.

In addition to Australia, there are also Welsh groups active in New Zealand, where (as in Australia) vast distances between settlements have prevented much communication between them. A Cymanfa Ganu is still held yearly in Auckland, and once every two years in Christchurch. Canterbury also has an active Welsh society. The sign "Welshtown" in a now deserted gold mining area of the South Island points to former Welsh settlement and activities in that area. New Zealand rugby teams still discuss the world-beating Welsh teams of the 1970's, and on a recent tour of the country, the author found that the story of the 1905 defeat of the Kiwis by Wales has become something of a legend.,

Sadly, unlike the Quebecois of Canada, fearful of losing their distinct identity, but who have a French "homeland" across the sea to replenish and sustain them, the overseas Welsh do not have the luxury of a strong, heavily-populated Welsh heartland where the language obtains pride of place and is universally spoken. Consequently Welsh men and women, wherever they reside, must do much more to help preserve their own homeland and to ensure that the language and culture of Wales does not soon disappear into the Celtic mists, never to be revived as a living, breathing natural entity.

The overseas Welsh, can keep in touch with their homeland and with St David societies in their adopted countries *through Yr Enfys* (The Rainbow) the magazine of Wales International, but they must heed the words of such fighters for the cause as Dafydd Iwan, who reminds us that he knows what is "right and proper" for the survival of his beloved land. For the Welsh in the United States, Canada, Australia, New Zealand and Patagonia, it is heartening that Wales now has its own Assembly.

Chapter Twelve: Some Famous Welsh Men and Women

The list of men and women from Wales who have excelled in their chosen field is a long one; they are found in every field of human endeavor. Two of Wales' brightest contemporaries are Robyn Lewis, the Archdruid and author of the *New Legal Dictionary;* and Dr. Rowan Williams, the Archbishop of Canterbury. Most well known, in this day and age, are the entertainers — the movie stars and singers who were born in Wales who have become world famous.

To name just a few of this distinguished and talented company we have the creator of reggae, Bob Marley (born to a Welsh father and Jamaican mother); Opera stars Gwyneth Jones and Margaret Price; Charlotte Church, the youngest singer ever to top the British classical music charts; Aled Jones, the former boy soprano, now having a successful career with the B.B.C.; golden-voiced, ever-young Shirley Bassey, from Cardiff's Tiger Bay; the irrepressible Tom Jones (depicted: "Tom the Voice" from Pontypridd), Terry Jones of "Monty Python" fame; Dorothy Squires, Britain's sweetheart from Pontyberem; Petula Clark, raised in Merthyr, with best-selling records in Britain and the U.S; husky-voiced Bonnie Tyler, from Swansea, with a huge following in pop music; Dafydd Iwan, ever-popular Welsh-language folk singer and former political activist; Allan Jones and his son, Jack, along with Thomas L. Thomas from the Welsh coal mining area of Scranton, Pennsylvania.

Modern Welsh Rock has given us such groups as Catatonia, Super Furry Animals, Stereophonics, and Manic Street Preachers to name a few. In the world of Opera and classical music, Wales has produced Dame Gwyneth Jones, Delme Bryn Jones, Dame Margaret Price, the incomparable Bryn Terfel, the late much-loved Geraint Evans; the tenors Dennis O'Neil and Stuart Burrows, all internationally famous. Worl-class harpists include Osian Ellis, Catrin Finch, (harpist to the

Prince of Wales), Llio Rydderch, Elinor Bennett, the late Nansi Richards (Queen of the gypsy-style harpists) and Eldra Jarman.

Composers and musicians include Joseph Parry, Ivor Novello (David Ivor Davies), Geraint Bowen, Michael Lewis (who composed the music for many Hollywood films), Walford Davies, Hadyn James, Karl Jenkins, Alun Hoddinott, Owain Arwel Hughes, Mansel Thomas, Karl Jenkins, and William Mathias. Famous in the United States was Dilwyn Owen Jones, "Jones the Jazz." We also acknowledge four of the many great hymn writers produced by Wales in William Williams "Pantycelyn", the incomparable mystic Ann Griffiths, Caradog Roberts, and Daniel Protheroe.

Wales has given us politicians and statesmen Thomas Jefferson, President of the United States (who stated that his ancestors came from the foot of Mt. Snowdon in Wales); David Lloyd George, Prime Minister of Great Britain; William Morris Hughes, the "Little Digger," Prime Minister of Australia; Charles Evans Hughes, Chief Justice of the United States Supreme Court; Robert Owen, U.S. Mineworkers' Union leader John L. Lewis; William Abraham (Mabon); influential British parliamentarians Roy Jenkins, James Callaghan, Hugh Dalton, Lord Howe, and Enoch Powell (for better or worse); the highly respected Jim Griffiths, first Secretary of State for Wales; and fiery Aneurin Bevan, father of Britain's Welfare state.

There have been many famous Welsh Americans in addition to Thomas Jefferson. They include Joshua Humphries, designer of frigates for the American navy, including the *Constitution* ("Old Ironsides") who can rightly be called "The Father of the U.S. Navy." We must also include Robert Morris, without whose financial support the Revolution would have surely failed. Prolific inventor Oliver Evans, who introduced automation to flour milling and who may have also invested the first steam driven automobile; John Griffiths, legendary shipbuilder whose beautifully designed clippers broke world records; Charles Evan Hughes, US Secretary of State, and Chief Justice of the US Supreme Court, and James J. Griffith, after whom Griffith Peak, Los Angeles is named.

The film industry gave us Ray Milland, Anthony Hopkins and Richard Burton, all from the same area of South Wales. They are joined by Catherine Zeta Jones from Swansea (seen here with Hopkins), Mervin Johns and his daughter Glynis; Ioan Gruffudd from Cardiff, Hugh Griffith from Anglesey; much beloved Edmund Gwenn, Hollywood's most famous and beloved Santa Claus, from Glamorgan; tough guy Stanley Baker, from the Rhondda; Timothy Dalton (James Bond), from Colwyn Bay; Jonathan Pryce, from Holywell; Sian Phillips, glamorous star of stage, screen, and television; and actress Rachel Roberts; and Emlyn Williams (dramatist, stage actor, and movie star). London born Bob Hope was the son of a lady from Swansea.

Britain's stage has been graced by comedian Tommy Cooper (with his trademark red fez); Tessie O' Shea (Two Ton Tessie); Harry Secombe, singer and comedian; and Dawn French, star of many BBC television series.

The world of international sports is well represented by some great Welsh athletes. They include: Harry Llewelyn and his Olympic Gold Medal winning horse Foxhunter; Tanni Grey-Thompson, world wheelchair athletic champion, winner of five Olympic Golds; Lyn Davies ("Lyn the Leap," former world record holder and Olympic champion in the Long Jump); Christian Malcolm, Colin Jackson, both world record holders in sprinting and hurdles; Steve Jones, who broke the world record in the Marathon; John Disley, Olympic steeplechase champion. We must not forget Col. Harry Llewellyn and *Foxhunter,* world champion horse and rider, who won the Olympic Gold at Helsinki in 1952. We must not forget Major Walter Wingfield, of North Wales, inventor of Lawn Tennnis.

Wales gave us some fine boxing world champions including one who is considered the greatest in his division, Jimmy Wilde "the

Mighty Atom," but also world champions Freddie Welsh, Tommy Farr, Howard Winstone, Jim Driscoll Dai Dower, and Joe Calzaghe, called "the terminator," world champion and undefeated middleweight (depicted: Tommy Farr and Joe Louis).

Rugby League gave us Billy Boston, one of the best try scorers ever, and Jim Sullivan, the most dominant player in the League. Rugby Union players include the following: Neil Jenkins, the highest points scorer in the history of international rugby; Gerald Davies, with the dazzling side step; Mervyn Davies, "Merv the Swerve"; Phil Bennett; Cliff Morgan; Gareth Edwards, voted the "best rugby player ever"; J.P.R. Williams, and Shane Williams.

Association Football (Soccer) perhaps the world's most popular spectator sport, has also been graced by many super stars from Wales, they include Billy Meredith, who helped beat England when he was 48 years old; John Charles "the Gentle Giant," revered in Italy, where he was a leading player for Juventus; Ian Rush, record goal scorer with Liverpool; Ryan Giggs, of the Manchester United; Craig Bellamy and Gary Speed, of Newcastle United: super centre-forward Trevor Ford, of Cardiff, Jack Kelsey, matchless goal keeper with Arsenal; stalwart half back Mike England; Mark Hughes, exceptional player and manager; Ivor Allchurch "the golden boy" of British football, and his team mate at Swansea, Cliff Jones, later at Tottenham. For many years the world's highest transfer fee belonged to Bryn Jones. To top off this list, we have the internationally known rugby referee Derek Bevan.

Welsh people can be successful businessmen. To name a few: David Davies, of Llandinam, canal and port builder; Howard Springer, head of Sony International; Terry Matthews, chief executive of many corporations and developer of Celtic Manor Complex. David Thomas, "the father of the American anthracite iron industry." Richard Parry Jones, Chief Technical Officer for Ford Motor company "known as "Ford's Secret Weapon."

In other areas, the Welsh have been prominent: Ernest Alfred Jones, an all-time great in psychoanalysis, worked closely with Carl Jung to pioneer research in that field. Physicists John Meurig Thomas, Frank Llewellyn Jones, and Tudor Bowden Jones have kept the Welsh flag flying in their internationally known endeavors, as have geologist

Owen Thomas Jones, scientist Alun D.W. Jones. A major figure in the field of wireless telegraphy and the telephone was Sir William H. Preece, from Caernarfon.

Famous Welsh explorers include H.M. Stanley, who discovered Livingstone in Africa; David Thompson, "that Welshman," who mapped one fifth of the North American continent, and John Thomas Evans who explored the Upper Mississippi and whose maps were used by Lewis and Clark. Welsh architects include William Clough Ellis, designer of Portmeirion, American Frank Lloyd Wright (born to a Welsh mother), and Welsh American Robert Trent Jones, designer of some of the world's great golf courses.

World-class authors include Bishop Morgan, O.M.Edwards, Dylan Thomas (depicted), Henry Vaughan, Jan Morris, Richard Llewellyn, W.H. Davies, Emlyn Williams, R.S.Thomas, Emyr Humphries, Kate Roberts, Jack Jones, Saunders Lewis, John Ceiriog Hughes, Gwyn Jones, John Davies, and many other novelists, short story writers, and poets. Welsh painters include Richard Wilson, who helped found the Royal Academy, and Augustus John and his sister Gwen.

To finish, and this list is far from complete, we dare mention that three of the most feared pirates who ever sailed the Seven Seas were Welsh: Bartholemew Roberts, known as *Black Bart*, the first to fly the Skull and Crossbones flag; Captain Henry Morgan, perhaps the most famous of them all, of the Golden Age of Piracy; and Howell Davies, "the Cavalier Prince of Pirates."

In addition, we must not forget immigrant Judge Edward J. Blythin's shenanigans during the notorious Sam Sheppard Trial that helped radically change US court procedures. Finally, to end this role call of the famous and not so famous, it is only fair to mention Llewelyn Morris Humphries, "Murray the Hump," was Al Capone's chief lieutenant and organizer.

Chapter Twelve: Conclusion, the Past, Present, and Future

The tiny country of Wales has proved itself. It is a country determined to survive as a cultural entity despite having been treated for so long as a mere minor, troublesome adjunct to its powerful neighbor. For hundreds of years, this large neighbor England has wished to ignore the small Western province, with its ancient traditions, its tricky, indecipherable language and customs (and perhaps even trickier, indecipherable people).

For generation after generation, in school after school, Welsh children were made familiar with the English poetry of Chaucer, but not the Welsh poetry of Dafydd ap Gwilym; that of Wordsworth, but not that of Ceiriog. They listened to the accomplishments of Alfred the Great, but were not told of those of Hywel Da. They were encouraged to read of the military exploits of Edward the Black Prince, but not those of Llywelyn ap Gruffudd.

Welsh children thrilled to the heroics of Hereward battling the Normans to preserve his Saxon heritage. The exploits of Owain Glyndwr, battling the armies of England to save his Welsh nation were glossed over or hardly mentioned. The same children studied the joys of French literature, but not those of living Celtic; the history of the Union Jack, but never that of the Red Dragon. Worst of all, Welsh children were forbidden to speak their native language in the Board Schools set up by Act of Parliament in 1889, and it was only in recent history that the teaching of Welsh was allowed.

In 1773, Rhys Jones wrote the following:

> *God has shown more love and favour to the Welsh than to almost any other nation under the sun...Although we were conquered by the Romans, and driven by the Saxons from the lowlands of England to the Welsh highlands, and late conquered by the Normans; and although laws were passed specifically to delete our*

> *language totally from the face of the earth yet the Most High has given us strength and resilience to withstand all the incursions of our enemies, however frequent they have been, and to retain our language and some of our possessions, also, despite them all; and let us hope that we shall remain so for ever more.*

Thanks to the pride installed by the flying of the Red Dragon, the continuance of such Welsh traditions as the Eisteddfod, the Noson Lawen and the Gymanfa Ganu, and perhaps, most important of all, its own Assembly, Wales endures. The opening of the New Wales Millenium Centre in the Fall of 2004 put its national capital Cardiff on the world stage. The Centre is home to seven cultural organizations including the Welsh National Opera and will symbolize Wales's important contributions to the arts and to music as well as its resurgence as a nation, at least freeing itself from dependence upon its powerful neighbour. As Dafydd Iwan so searchingly reminds us in his patriotic song *Yma O Hyd*, "In spite of all and everything, we are still here."

Appendix One: Important Dates in Welsh History

1000 BC:	The Iron Age
500-100 BC:	The Arrival of the Celts
43-383 AD:	Roman Britain
383:	The withdrawal of Macsen's Legions
400-600:	The Anglo-Saxon Invasions
516:	The Battle of Mount Badon (in which Arthur defeated a Saxon army).
55-650:	The Division of Britain into the Britonnic West, the Teutonic East, and the Gaelic North.
425-664:	The Age of the Celtic Saints
c.600:	The Welsh language begins its written history.
615:	The Battle of Chester and the separation of Wales from the Northern kingdoms.
633:	Wales begins as a separate cultural unit (to be known as Cymru).
664:	The Death of Cadwaladr ends the hope of the Britons to take back their lands.
784:	Offa's Dyke is constructed to separate the Welsh and English peoples.
844-877:	The reign of Rhodri Mawr unites Wales.
900-950:	The reign of Hywel Dda (Howell the Good).

937:	The victory of Athelstan over the Celtic alliance at Brunanburgh.
1039-63:	The Kingdom of Gruffudd ap Llywelyn: a united Wales.
1066-77:	The coming of the Normans to Wales.
1090:	*The Life of St. David* by Rhygyfarch.
1137-1170:	The reign of Owain Gwynedd "Prince of Wales."
1169:	Prince Madog arrives in the New World (according to legend).
1176:	An Eisteddfod is held at Aberteifi.
1200-1240:	Reunification of Wales under Llywelyn ap Iorwerth.
1222-1283:	Rebellion of Llywelyn ap Gruffudd
1277:	The Treaty of Aberconwy and the beginning of Edwards lst's castles.
1282:	Prince Llywelyn slain at Cilmeri, Powys.
1284:	The Statute of Rhuddlan ended Welsh hopes of independence.
14th C.	Literary revival: *The Mabinogion,* the Poets of the Gentry, and Dafydd ap Gwilym.
1294-1400:	Rebellion under Owain Glyndwr.
1402:	Penal Laws enacted against Wales.
1404:	Glyndwr summons a parliament at Machynlleth.

1409:	The Charter of Brecon further punishes the people of Wales.
1485:	The Battle of Bosworth brings the first of Tudors to the throne of England
1536:	The Act of Union permanently joins Wales to England and proposes to wipe out the Welsh language.
155l:	In his *Kynniver Lyth a Ban*, William Salesbury translates the main texts of the English Prayer Book.
1557:	Salesbury translates the *New Testament* and *The Book of Common Prayer* into Welsh.
1567:	Caerwys, Flintshire, holds its second eisteddfod under royal patronage .
157l:	Jesus College, Oxford is founded.
1573:	Humphrey Lhuyd publishes the first Map of Wales.
1585:	A collection of religious texts, *Yn Llyvyr Hwnn* (In This Book), published by John Prys of Brecon, is the first book published in the Welsh language.
1588:	The translation of the *Holy Bible* is completed by Bishop William Morgan.
162l:	Poet William Cynwal publishes his *Salmau Can*, used as a hymnal for over a century.
1650:	Act for the Better Propagation and Preaching of the Gospel prepares the way for a religious revival.

1662:	The Act of Uniformity leads many Welsh congregations into emigrating to America.
1664:	The Conventicle Act continues the move to the New World.
1681:	The publication of *Canwyll y Cymry* (Candle of the Welsh) by Rhys Pritchard does much to sustain the language.
1681:	William Penn is granted Propriety Rights to New Wales, later called Pennsylvania.
1699:	The Society for the Propagation of Christian Knowledge is founded by Sir John Phillips of Pembrokeshire.
1718:	A printing press is set up at Trefhedyn, Cardiganshire to publish Welsh books.
1729:	The St.David's Society of Philadelphia is founded.
1740:	Griffith Jones publishes *Welsh Piety* and sets up circulating schools and evening classes to make the Welsh a literate people.
1751:	The Honourable Society of the Cymmrodorion is founded in London.
1760:	Iron master John Guest arrives in Dowlais.
176l:	John Wilkinson sets up his factory in Bersham, Wrexham to begin an industrial revolution in North Wales.
1762:	William Williams (Pantycelyn) publishes his collection of hymns.

1766:	Copper ore is mined at Parys, Anglesey.
1770:	The *Peter Williams Bible* is published.
1770:	The Gwyneddigion is founded in London.
1776:	Richard Price publishes his *The Nature of Civil Liberty,* supporting the rights of the American Colonies.
1778:	Thomas Pennant's *Tours in Wales* begins a flood of travelers to North Wales.
1782:	David Williams advocates political reform in his *Letters on Political Liberty.*
1784:	The process of puddling iron is brought to Merthyr Tydfil, to make it a center of industry and to transform the Valleys.
1784:	Thomas Charles sets up a successful Sunday School movement in North Wales.
1792:	The eisteddfod is revived in London.
1793:	The first Welsh periodical is published as *Cylchgrawn Cymmraeg* (Welsh Magazine).
1794:	The Glamorgan Canal links Merthyr to Cardiff, to transform the city.
1797:	The last invasion of mainland Britain is attempted at Fishguard, but repelled.
1804:	The first weekly newspaper in Wales is published in Swansea as *The Cambrian.*

1804:	Trevithick's revolutionary steam locomotive to be run on rails succeeds at Penydareen, Merthyr
1804:	The Swansea and Oystermouth Railway begins an operation lasting until 1960.
1806:	The hymns of Ann Griffiths are published.
18ll:	Wales breaks from the Anglican Church by establishing the Calvinistic Methodists.
1814:	Seren y Gomer, published at Swansea is the first Welsh language weekly.
1819:	The Gorsedd comes to Wales at Carmarthen.
1826:	Telford completes the suspension bridges over the Conwy and the Menai.
1830:	The first trade union in Britain, the Friendly Associated Coalminers' Union, was formed at Bagillt, Flintshire,
1831	The Merthyr Rising is suppressed and Dic Penderyn hanged.
1834:	Robert Owen sets up the Grand National Consolidated Trade Union to have a major impact on future trade unionism.
1837:	At Ynycedwyn David Thomas uses the hot blast to smelt iron ore with anthracite
1838-49:	*The Mabinogion* is published in English by Lady Llanover (Charlotte Guest).
1839:	The Bute Dock is completed at Cardiff to to export coal sent down from the Valleys.

1839: The Rebecca Riots in South West Wales.

1839: A Chartist Riot takes place at Llanidloes, followed by the great Chartist March in Newport that is brutally crushed.

1841: Cardiff is linked to Bristol by rail.

1842-47: The Royal Commission into the State of Education in Wales condemns the language.

1848: Trinity College, Carmarthen, is founded.

1849: The first Welsh religious service is held in Australia at Burra.

1851: *Y Drych,* Welsh-American newspaper begins in New York City.

1859: *Baner ac Amserau Cymru* begins its major impact on Welsh life for over a century.

1861: The first truly National Eisteddfod is is held in Aberdare.

1865: The Welsh Colony of Patagonia is founded.

1867: The Great Reform Act creates 60,000 new voters in Wales and shatters the power of the landed gentry and industrialists.

1869: *The Western Mail* is founded in Cardiff.

1870: Board Schools are set up in which the language of instruction is English.

1872: The first University College of Wales opens in Aberystwyth.

1873:	The Monmouthshire and South Wales Coal-Owners' Association is set up to combat Trade unions.
1877:	The Cambrian Miners' Association is founded in the Rhondda Valley
1881:	The Welsh Rugby Union is established.
1881:	The Welsh Sunday Closing Act is the first piece of government legislation designed specifically for Wales.
1885:	At Aberdare Eisteddfod, Isaac Davies founds the *Society for the Utilization of the Welsh language* (Cymdeithas yr Iaith Gymraeg).
1886:	Cymru Fydd (Wales of the Future) is founded in Bala by Tom Ellis.
1889:	The Miners' Federation of Great Britain is founded at Newport.
1890:	David Lloyd George is elected to Parliament
1891:	Owen M. Edwards launches the monthly magazine *Cymru.*
1891:	The McKinley Tariff, passed in the U.S, hurts the Welsh tinplate industry.
1893:	The University of Wales Charter allowed Welsh colleges to grant degrees.
1898:	The South Wales Miners' Federation is set up with Mabon as its first president.
1900:	Keir Hardie is elected to Parliament.

1900:	The defeat of the railway workers in the *Taff Vale Railway Case* fosters the growth of the Labour Party.
1900:	*The Great Unrest* ushered in a period of strikes and industrial unrest. The Penrhyn quarry workers stayed out for three years.
1904:	The Great Religious Revival begins in Cardigan and sweeps through Wales.
1905:	Cardiff is elevated to the status of a city.
1907:	The National National Museum of Wales (at Cardiff) and the National Library of Wales at Aberystwyth) are opened.
1910:	The Tonypandy Riots brings in the London Police sent by Winston Churchill.
1913:	An explosion in the Senghenydd mine kills 439 men after warnings had been ignored.
1914-18:	The First World War creates a shared British identity.
1916:	Lloyd George becomes Prime Minister.
1917:	The Birkenhead (Cheshire) eisteddfod honors poet Hedd Wynn, killed in France shortly before.
1920:	The University College of Swansea is founded.
1920:	The Church of Wales is disestablished.
1922:	The Welsh League of Youth (*Urdd Gobaith Cymru)* is founded.

1925:	Plaid Cymru is founded at Pwllheli.
1927:	Colleg Harlech opens its doors to working men and women.
1932:	The Welsh language newspaper *Y Cymro* begins.
1934:	The Gresford Disaster kills 266 miners.
1935:	The first radio broadcast in Welsh begin.
1936:	"The Fire at Penyberth" is started by three members of Plaid Cymru to become a "Cause Celebre" in the fight for Wales.
1939-45:	The Second World War puts a hold on any aspirations for Welsh nationhood.
1945:	Welshmen Aneurin Bevan and James Griffiths work to pass the National Insurance Act.
1947:	The Wales Gas Board is established.
1947:	A Welsh language primary school begins at Llanelli.
1948:	The Council of Wales is established through the efforts of James Griffiths.
1955:	Cardiff is selected as the capital of Wales.
1956:	Two secondary schools are set up in Flintshire to teach through the medium of Welsh.
1957:	Trywerin Valley is drowned for a reservoir.
1962:	A new *Cymdeithas yr Iaith Cymraeg* is founded.

1964: James Griffiths becomes the first Secretary of State for Wales.

1966: Gwynfor Evans is elected to Parliament as the first Member for Plaid Cymru.

1966: A disaster at Aberfan buries 144 children and their teachers under a mountain of waste.

1967: The Welsh Language Act gives legal status to Welsh for the first time.

1967: The Gittins Report recommends that Welsh children be given the opportunity to be reasonably bilingual at the primary stage.

1969: Charles is invested as the Prince of Wales at Caernarfon Castle.

1971: The Welsh Nursery School Movement (*Sefydlu Mudiad Ysgolion Meithrin)* is founded.

1974: Local government reorganization creates eight Welsh counties from the original thirteen.

1974: Oaths of allegiance in Welsh are allowed in Parliament for the first time

1977: Radio Cymru and Radio Wales are established.

1979: A Referendum for a Welsh Assembly is defeated.

1982: A Welsh language television Channel is begun.

1997: A successful Referendum gives Wales its own Assembly with a measure of self-government after centuries of domination by Westminster.

2004: *Y Drych* merges with *Ninnau* to form a single newspaper for the Welsh of North America.

2004: At Buffalo, New York State, the North American Welsh Gymanfa Ganu, now renamed the Festival Of Wales, celebrates its 75th anniversary

2010: Government proposals to give more validity to the Welsh language

Appendix Two: The Welsh Alphabet (Y Wyddor).

Very few modern European languages are derived from *Celtic*. In mainland Britain, at least for a few hundred years after the Roman victories on mainland Europe, the Celtic speaking people managed to hold on to much of their customs and especially to their distinctive languages, one of which has survived today as *Welsh*.

This language, used throughout most of Britain at the time of the Roman invasions (except in the far north where Pictish survived for a while) was derived from a branch of Celtic known as *Brythonic*; it later gave rise to Welsh, Cornish and Breton. These differ from other Celtic languages derived from the branch known as *Goidelic*: namely, Irish, Scots, and Manx Gaelic (now confined to a western fringe in Ireland, to the north and west of Scotland, or to the history books as an extinct spoken tongue).

The Welsh Alphabet has much in common with other Celtic languages, though its modern orthography makes it resemble those Continental languages stemming from Latin, such as French and Spanish rather than those stemming from Germanic, such as English.

Welsh has twenty-eight letters.: seven vowels, twenty-one consonants (with eleven diphthongs):

The following letters do not appear in the Welsh alphabet, except in modern borrowings from English: j, k, q, v, x, and z. Ironically, the most common surname in Wales, by far, is Jones. It seems to have come about in the Tudor period when Welsh families took English names or were given them by official government scribes and record keepers unable to, or unwilling to, register Welsh names. Welsh families adopted English names or took those names from the Bible that closely resembled their own.

Pronunciation:

The Seven Vowels: a, e, i, o, u, w, y.

A as in Man. Welsh words am, ap, ap

E as in bet, or echo. Welsh words: gest, enaid (enide)

I as in pita or pizza. Welsh words: mi, min (meen)

O as in lot or mow. Welsh words: hoffi, dod (dode) bob (bobe)

U as in pita. Welsh words: Cymru (Kumree) Ganu (Ganee)

W as in tomb. Welsh words: cwm (Koom) yw (you) or as in bus. Welsh word bws (bus).

Y as in the y in myrrh or in the final sound of Betty. Welsh words: yr (ur), yn (un) fry (vree), byd (beed).

All vowels can be lengthened by the addition of a circumflex (^) called in Welsh tô bach (little roof). Welsh words: tân (taan), lân (laan).

Diphthongs: ae, ai, au, aw, eu, oe, ou, wy.

Ae, ai, and au are all pronounced as the English eye or hide. Welsh words: mae (my), Ninnau (Nineye), arfau (arveye), tai (tye).

Aw is pronounced as in the English word *cow*. Welsh words: mawr (mowr), prynhawn (prunhown), wawr (wour). lawr (lour).

Eu and ei are pronounces the same as English a as in *hay*. Welsh words: eu (ey), deil (dayle). In the U.S. there is a tendency to pronounce ei as *eye*. Welsh word deisiau (dyeshy). In N. Wales, this is Deeshuh.

Ew has no equivalent in English (except perhaps for the Midland *you* (yeooh). Welsh words: mewn (may-oon). The Welsh words are not drawn out but contracted.

Oe is similar to English *oy.* Welsh words: Oedd (oythe), Croeso (croyso), troed (troyd).

Ow is the same as the English *tow*. Welsh words: rhown (rhone), glôwr (glo'r).

Wy has no equivalent in English. Welsh words wy (oowee), hwyl (hooil, wyf (ooiv).

Ywy is pronounced as in English *ow* (cow). Welsh words: Bywyd (bowid), tywyll (towith).

Consonants: the following are pronounced as in English: b, c, d, h, l, m, n. p, ph, r, s, t, and th with the exception that h is always pronounced, never silent and th is always pronounced as in the English think, never as in seethe.

C is always pronounced as in English cat, never as in English since or *cypher*. Welsh words: canu (canny).

Ch is pronounced as in Scottish *loch*, or German *ach,* never as in English *Church*. Welsh words: bach, chi.

Dd is pronounces as the English th in the word *seethe, them.* Welsh words: dydd (deethe), bydd (beethe).

F is pronounces as the English v in the words *very, vile*. Welsh words: fan (van), fy (vuh), fawr (vowr).

Ff corresponds to English f or ph. Welsh words: Ffynnon (funon), Ffaith (fithe, Ffôn (phone).

G is pronounced as in English *goat* or gore, never as in *George*. Welsh words: ganu (ganee), ganaf (ganav).

Ng is pronounced as the ng in Long Island, or as in *finger*. Welsh words: nglanhau (unglanhigh), ngrym (ungrim).

Th is pronounced as the English words *think, forth, thank*. Welsh words: gwaith (gwithe), arfaith (arvithe.

Ll has no equivalent in English. It is an aspirated l sound. (similar to the th sound followed by l). Welsh words: Llan (thlan), llawr (thlour), Llofnod (thlovnod).

Rh has no equivalent in English. It is pronounced by rolling the r and using the h sound (similar to the Scottish sound in perhaps). Welsh words: rhaff (hrraff), rhown (hrrown).

The National Anthem of Wales:
(Yr Anthem Genedlaethol)

Mae hen wlad fy nhadau	The old land of my fathers
Yn annwyl i mi.	Is dear to me.
Gwlad beirdd a chantorion	The land of bards and singers
Enwogion o fri	Highly renowned
Ei gwrol ryfelwyr	Its brave warriors
Gwladgarwyr tra mâd	Extremely fine patriots
Tros ryddid gollasant	For freedom they lost their blood eu gwaed
Cydgan (chorus):	
Gwlad, gwlad	My land, my land
Pleidiol wyf i'm gwlad.	I am pledged to my land.
Tra môr yn fur	While the sea is a wall
I'r bur hoff bau	To the dear, pure land
O bydded i'r hen iaith	O, let the Old language continue barhau

(Words by Evan James : Tr. by Peter N. Williams)

Gweddi'r Arglwydd (The Lord's Prayer)

Ein Tad, yr Hwn wyt yn y nefoedd

Sancteiddier dy enw

Deled dy deyrnas,

Gwneler dy ewyllys,

Megis yn y nef,

Felly ar y ddaear hefyd

Dyro I ni heddiw ein bara beunyddiol

A maddau i ni ein dyledion

Fel y maddeuwn ninnau i'n dyledwyr;

Ac nac arwain ni i brofedigaeth,

Eithr gwared ni rhag drwg

Canys eiddot Ti yw y deyrnas

A'r nerth, a'r gogoniant

Yn oes oesoedd.

Amen

About the Author

Peter N. Williams was born in Flintshire, North Wales. Brought up in the industrial town of Flint (Y Ffllint), he was educated at King's School, Chester, and University College, Swansea, South Wales, where he obtained an Honours degree in History and a Diploma in Education. After arriving in the U.S. in 1957, Peter served with the US Army in Germany, where he produced and directed entertainment for the Seventh Army Artillery Group. He then began a career as a teacher at Smyrna's John Bassett Moore High School, Brandywine High School, and Concord High School, Wilmington, Delaware, completing his M.A. and Ph.D. degrees at the University of Delaware. He taught English at the University before becoming Chairman of the English Department at Delaware Technical and Community College. During that time he performed with the Wilmington Drama League, the Breck's Mill Cronies, and the Delaware Dinner Theatre. For five years he was the leading writer on British history at Britannia.com and is now the editor/writer of *Celticinfo.com* and *The Eagle and the Dragon* (the NWAF quarterly).

Peter is on the Board of Directors of NWAF and the founder and current President of the Welsh Society of Delaware. He is an accomplished conductor of Gymanfaoedd Ganu and Nosweithiau Lawen, and has lectured on Wales and its language in three states and in Great Britain and Ireland. Peter was honored for his work on behalf of Wales and Welsh Americans by being elected to the Gorsedd of Bards of the Isle of Britain (white robe). He has also been honored by the St. David's Society of Philadelphia as Welshman of the Year.

Peter has written several books on Wales and the Welsh, including *The Sacred Places of Wales: a New Pilgrimage*; *The Seven Wonders of Wales; From Wales to the Lehigh: the David Thomas Story; The Eighth Wonder of Wales: the Survival of its Ancient Celtic Language*;

Wales and the Welsh: An Alphabetical Guide; The History of Wales in Verse, Your Welsh Heritage, and The Long,Hard Struggle: A History of Wales.

www.ingramcontent.com/pod-product-compliance
Lightning Source LLC
Chambersburg PA
CBHW031243280526
45784CB00004B/1699

* 9 7 8 0 5 5 7 4 3 7 3 8 2 *